A Treasure Worth Finding

90

*Devotions to bring
light to your path*

Seth Buckner

Seth Buckner
1608 Hwy 59 South
Jefferson, TX 75657
(903)665-8865

The contents of this book come from years of life and ministry. It is not our intent to claim originality with any quote or thought that could not readily be tied to an original source.

Cover art by Nadjib from Unsplash

Paperback ISBN 9798483268925

Hardback ISBN 9798496913843

Printed in the United States of America

This book is dedicated to the man who has loved me since I was born, and even before. Dad, thank you for always being there for me.

Table of Contents

1. A Treasure Worth Finding
2. The Old Bible
3. Hold The Bible High
   Gary Uit de Flesch
4. The Christian's Responsibility in Shaky Times
5. Can You Hear Me Now?
6. God Meant It for Good
7. Asking God for Hard Things
8. Worthless Doctors
9. The Difference Maker
10. Lions Are Not Pets
11. It Is Well with My Soul
12. Promotion of Praise
13. Facing Fear Fearlessly
14. Almost Persuaded
15. Time Travel
16. The Judge Gives Grace
17. Courageous Commitment
18. Why So Much Pain?
19. I Want to Be Appreciated
20. What Really Makes America Great
21. The Miracle of Freedom
22. A Pastor's Perspective of 9/11
23. The Church and Racism
24. The Little Engine That Could
25. God Cares for The Sparrows
26. What Were You Thinking?
27. Someone Is Watching
28. What The Bible Says About Wearing Mask
29. A Mom Worth Talking About
    Phyllis Buckner
30. The Influence of a Godly Mother
31. Letter to Mom
32. The Father's Importance
33. Think of Others
34. Finding Grace Everywhere
35. How Is Your Joy Count?
36. Fellowship With God
37. Prayer is Important
38. If You Love Me
39. Famous Lies

40. How Will You Be Remembered?
    Elmer Dacus
41. Don't Worry
42. Do You Have a Leak?
43. Eat Your Shoe and Keep Your Word
44. Love Is More Than a Day
45. Don't Let Your Love Get Cold
46. Snow Treasures
47. God and the Weather
48. Making a Difference
49. What Is Your Worldview?
50. A Golden Sacrifice
51. Celebrate the Timing
52. A Worthy Resurrection
53. Making Our Life Count
54. Oh, What a Savior!
55. An Example of Friendship
56. Giant Questions of Faith
57. A Wise Search
58. Is It Good to Walk?
59. Games People Play
60. The Horseshoe Crab
61. Shadows of Life
62. The Cupbearer Called
63. The Bible Says Jesus Is God
64. From The Diamond to The Bush
    Bobby Bonner
65. The Man Who Changed Lives
    Ben Kendrick
66. The Tract Man
    Bruce DeLange
67. Purity Pays
68. Protect Your Purity
69. Bleeding Scripture
70. Reaching The Whole World
71. Does Anyone Fast Anymore?
72. Giving or Receiving?
73. Lost Connection
74. How To Pray for Your Pastor
75. How To Pray for Your Church
76. We Are All Dedicated to Something
77. Thanks To God
78. Thanksgiving in a Pickle

79. Quarantined
80. Great Grandparents
81. Camouflage Christians
82. Opening Weekend
83. Reflecting Jesus in Our Race
84. Reflecting Jesus in Our Urgency
85. Reflecting Jesus in Our Vision
86. Why Read the Bible?
87. The Most Wonderful Time
88. Hurting Around the Christmas Tree
    Abigail Goodman
89. Running The Wrong Race
90. Finish Strong

Treasure Worth Finding

A treasure chest full of gold, jewelry, and other valuables worth $1 million was found in the Rocky Mountains, according to the late author and art dealer Forrest Fenn, who hid it more than a decade ago.

An estimated 350,000 treasure hunters were inspired to look for the valuable chest. The treasure was said to be north of Santa Fe, New Mexico, and many deciphered clues from Fenn's writing, including a 24-line poem published in his 2010 autobiography, "The Thrill of the Chase."

The state of Texas has an estimated $340 million in buried treasure, more than any other state in the United States. Across the state are countless stories and legends of buried loot. One cannot help but dream of finding some treasure and living a life of ease for the remainder of our days. Maybe we can strike it rich in our own backyards?

As much as we would like to dig up a box of gold from behind our tool shed, we should realize that it is highly unlikely. Fortunately, there is treasure to be found in our lives that has much greater value than a dump truck of diamonds.

If you have a copy of a Bible, you have a treasure book of knowledge. Just reading this Holy Book will reap great rewards! Revelation 1:3 says, "Blessed is he that readeth, and they that hear the words of this prophecy, and keep those things which are written therein: for the time is at hand." Queen Elizabeth II put it this way, "To what greater inspiration and counsel can we turn than to the imperishable truth to be found in this treasure house, the Bible?"

The Bible always tells the truth. It speaks to our heart honestly and penetrates our heart to meet our deepest needs. An abundance of stuff will never meet our need like Jesus will. Luke 12:21 says, "So is he that layeth up treasure for himself, and is not rich toward God."

William Penn said this, "Knowledge is the treasure of a wise man." A wise man will spend time soaking up the knowledge found in God's Word. Matthew 6:21 says, "For where your treasure is, there will your heart be also."

The Old Bible

How important is the Bible? Something so incredibly valuable can never be assigned a dollar amount. Romans 15:4 states, "For whatsoever things were written aforetime were written for our learning, that we through patience and comfort of the scriptures might have hope." Do you believe this? How often do you spend time exploring the pages of your Bible? Many years ago, when this pastor was a teenager, he penned the words to the following little poem called "The Old Bible."

> The Bible on the shelf lay,
> gathering dust day after day.
> It hadn't been touched in over a year,
> in no one's heart was it held dear.
> Mom and Dad were too busy to read.
> Besides, they didn't see the need.
> The kids followed their parent's way,
> so the Bible on the shelf stayed.
>
> The old Book was worn from much use,
> pages were stained, and the cover was loose.
> Grandmother had cherished every word,
> tears had washed it as her heart stirred.
> Now it is useless and ignored you see,
> gladly replaced by a big-screen TV.
> How do we refuse the Bible's need?
> Just lay it down and never read!

George Washington wrote, "It is impossible to rightly govern the world without God and the Bible." Andrew Jackson said, "That Book, sir, is the rock on which our republic rests." Abraham Lincoln stated, "I believe the Bible is the best gift God has ever given to man. All the good from the Savior of the world is communicated to us through this book."

The Bible is how God Himself speaks to us, so it is important that we take some time this week to hear it taught and to study it ourselves. Every page is valuable and worth our time and effort to learn its truths. "All scripture is given by inspiration of God, and is profitable..."

Hold The Bible High

Gary Uit de Flesch

Gary Uit de Flesch is a little-known pastor of a Baptist church in a small town in Minnesota. Most readers have never met him or even heard of him. Therefore, I want to tell you a little about him. For twenty-plus years he has been one of the most influential men in my life.

I met Brother Gary in the 1990's when he came to visit his daughter in Bible college. He was kind and encouraging and spoke to me strongly about my walk with God. This would become a trend through the coming years.

While visiting his house in my early 20's, it always felt like I was attending a Christian camp. We read the Bible in the morning and after every meal. We would spend extensive time reading the Bible in the evening. We would go to church and have a prayer and time in the Word and come straight home and do more!

Few people have I met in life who love their Bibles more, and who wanted to persuade others to do the same. I attribute much of my great love for the scriptures to the influence of this man. During a message he preached at the church I pastor, I committed to do family devotions with my family. By God's grace we have continued to do so for many years. His impact has been felt on his grandchildren, and I pray that someday his influence will continue with their children.

In 1 Samuel 18:18 David said to Saul, "Who am I? and what is my life, or my father's family in Israel, that I should be son in law to the king?" In a different context, I say, "Who am I, that I get to have Gary Uit de Flesch as a father-in-law?" Psalms 119:9 says, "Wherewithal shall a young man cleanse his way? by taking heed thereto according to thy word."

"For the word of God *is* quick, and powerful, and sharper than any twoedged sword, piercing even to the dividing asunder of soul and spirit, and of the joints and marrow, and *is* a discerner of the thoughts and intents of the heart." Hebrews 4:12

The Christians Responsibility in Shaky Times

What is our responsibility in these unusual days? Are you displeased with the leadership of our country? Are you displeased with the apathy of Christians around you? Are you displeased with the sin that is running unchecked in our society?

We all have things that displease us. Your list might be different than mine. The real question is this: what is our responsibility when we are displeased?

In first Samuel 8, the people came to Samuel and said, "You are old, and your kids are not good leaders. Make us a king so we can be like all the other nations." 1 Samuel 8:6 says, "But the thing displeased Samuel, when they said, Give us a king to judge us. And Samuel prayed unto the LORD."

Displease means "to tremble or to quiver." Have you ever been so upset that you almost start to shake? Sometimes bad things happen when people get this way. What is our responsibility in these times of our lives?

Samuel did something that every Christian should automatically do when shaken. Sadly, we do not do it as often as we should. Samuel turned immediately to the Lord.

What do we do in times of crisis? What do we do when people question our qualification? What do we do when everyone and everything seems to be coming against us? We should turn to the One that can make a real difference! Psalm 40:2 says, "He brought me up also out of an horrible pit, out of the miry clay, and set my feet upon a rock, and established my goings."

The Lord heard Samuel's prayer, and gave him the answers that he needed. He calmed Samuel by reminding him of the bigger picture. Samuel then did exactly what the Lord told him to do, which is the best decision a believer can make.

Being right with God is the Christian's responsibility in shaky times. Are you right with Him? It is time! Romans 13:11 says, "And that, knowing the time, that now it is high time to awake out of sleep: for now is our salvation nearer than when we believed."

Can You Hear Me Now?

Most people believe they are better listeners than they really are. Often friends are just waiting for you to take a breath so they can share their own words which are much more important. John Wayne put it this way, "People are short on ears and long on mouth."

Proverbs 1:5 says, "A wise man will hear, and will increase learning; and a man of understanding shall attain unto wise counsels." This verse tells us that a smart person will be a listening to other smart people to improve themselves.

It is possible to hear someone talk but not listen. One of the primary reasons given for failed relationships is the lack of listening. Two men were talking one day in front of the grocery store. One of them said, "My wife talks to herself a lot." His friend answered, "Mine does too, but she doesn't know it. She thinks I'm listening."

Don't be too proud to listen to people who want to help you be a better person. This is wisdom, and a sensible person will gladly hear wisdom. Proverbs 23:9 says, "Speak not in the ears of a fool: for he will despise the wisdom of thy words."

Listening is a key ingredient of church attendance. A wise person would stop sneaking peeks at their social media pages or checking sports scores and pay attention to the speaker. Unfortunately, church goers are often more excited about the benediction than the opening prayer. What did your pastor share last Sunday?

Don't be like the people in Zechariah 7:11: "But they refused to hearken, and pulled away the shoulder, and stopped their ears, that they should not hear." Jesus said, "He that hath ears to hear, let him hear." How about we all work on our listening skills this week.

"Let us hear the conclusion of the whole matter: Fear God, and keep his commandments: for this *is* the whole *duty* of man." Ecclesiastes 12:13

"It takes a great man to be a good listener."— Calvin Coolidge

God Meant It for Good

Joseph's life was a series of trials and misfortune. His life was marked by many valleys and few mountains. As a child he was mistreated badly by his siblings. The Bible details the hatred and cruelty of his brothers. Slavery is one of man's greatest evils, and Joseph was made a slave. Prison is hard enough when you are guilty, but Joseph went to prison because of a lie. In prison he sat forgotten for years.

On the other hand, the story of Joseph takes a different turn. He is taken out of prison and lifted to a position of power and prominence in Egypt. Joseph is reunited with his brothers, and God uses Joseph to bring his brothers to repentance. Joseph has a joyful and tearful reunion with his father.

The one thing that holds true through all the highs and lows: God meant it for good! One of the greatest attributes that Joseph displayed was the faith to realize this. Joseph's brothers were terrified that he would retaliate against them, but Joseph refused. Genesis 50:19-20; "And Joseph said unto them, Fear not: for am I in the place of God? But as for you, ye thought evil against me; but God meant it unto good, to bring to pass, as it is this day, to save much people alive."

In our life there are no accidents. There is no such thing as a coincidence. The good and bad things in your life are the working of the will of God. Psalm 135:5-6 says, "For I know that the Lord is great, and that our Lord is above all gods. Whatsoever the Lord pleased, that did He in heaven, and in earth, in the seas, and all deep places."

Do you have peace that God is active in every part of your life? Are there some things and places that you cannot reconcile? I encourage you to bring those things to Christ and let Him help you. Will you do it? Why not ask Him to give you the peace that is missing in your life?

> "Wherefore also we pray always for you, that our God
> would count you worthy of *this* calling, and fulfil all
> the good pleasure of *his* goodness, and the work of
> faith with power." 2 Thessalonians 1:11

Asking God for Hard Things.

Have you ever asked for something that seemed impossible? Many problems and goals seem like they can never be overcome, but God is able to do more than we ask or even think. Mark 10:27 says, "With men it is impossible, but not with God: for with God all things are possible."

2 Kings 2:9-10 says, "And it came to pass, when they were gone over, that Elijah said unto Elisha, Ask what I shall do unto thee, before I be taken away from thee. And Elisha said, I pray thee, let a double portion of thy spirit rest upon me. And he said, thou hast asked a hard thing: nevertheless if thou see me when I am taken from thee, it shall be so unto thee."

The prophet Elisha had asked a hard thing, but was it too hard for God? No way! Elisha did twice as many miracles as Elijah, including the last one long after he had passed away. A dead man returned to life as his body touched the bones of Elisha. Now that is a hard thing!

There is a song that says, "God can do anything, anything, anything; God can do anything but fail." Do not put limitations on the Lord, even when you do not think something is possible. Jeremiah 33:3 says, "Call unto me, and I will answer thee, and shew thee great and mighty things, which thou knowest not."

Do not be fearful to pray an impossible prayer and ask for the hard things. God wants to do great things with our simple faith in Him. Hebrews 11:6 says, "But without faith it is impossible to please him: for he that cometh to God must believe that he is, and that he is a rewarder of them that diligently seek him."

"The word impossible is not in my dictionary" — Napoleon Bonaparte

"We would accomplish many more things if we did not think of them as impossible." – Vince Lombardi

"And Jesus looking upon them saith, With men *it is* impossible, but not with God: for with God all things are possible." Mark 10:27

Worthless Doctors

There is no doubt that there are great doctors, but there are always some who could be considered worthless. Almost everyone could mention a name whom they could put into the bad doctor category.

Maybe they are worthless in your eyes because of poor treatment, high prices, misdiagnosis, or long waits. Someone recently mentioned that they could burn their money and get more use than spending it at their doctor. "At least I could get a little heat."

Job 13:4 talks about worthless doctors: "But ye are forgers of lies, ye are all physicians of no value." It is a helpless feeling to feel cheated by the one who should give comfort and healing.

If you face defeat and depression about the treatment you are receiving, or hurt from loss or addiction, there is good news. Jesus is the "Great Physician" who cares for you spiritually and physically.

Jesus said in Luke 4:18, "The Spirit of the Lord is upon me, because he hath anointed me to preach the gospel to the poor; he hath sent me to heal the brokenhearted, to preach deliverance to the captives, and recovering of sight to the blind, to set at liberty them that are bruised."

Jesus will never overcharge, and He will always give the right diagnosis. He knows the cure! He is readily available and is just one simple prayer away. There is no waiting room, and no one must wait for an audience with the Great Physician!

Luke 5:31-32 says, "And Jesus answering said unto them, They that are whole need not a physician; but they that are sick. I came not to call the righteous, but sinners to repentance." The Great Physician is looking for new patients—He will never turn you away. Will you visit Him today?

> "Christ is a substitute for everything, but nothing is a substitute for Christ." — Henry Allen Ironside

> "He is the best physician who is the most ingenious inspirer of hope." — Samuel Taylor Coleridge

The Difference Maker

We are all familiar with the story of the virgin Mary. The Bible account of her life and Jesus' birth is read by millions every year, and the name Mary is given to countless people. Mary receives a special visitor, the angel Gabriel sent from God to ask her to make a very difficult decision. This decision would not only change her life but would change the direction of all humanity.

Her answer to God's request in Luke 1:38 was simple: "And Mary said, Behold the handmaid of the Lord; be it unto me according to thy word..."

Mary was swift to follow what God wanted. As soon as Gabriel finished his message, she agreed without hesitation. She was willing to surrender her life completely to the Lord's will without asking for time to think about it. Mary called herself a handmaid, which is basically an indentured servant with a lifetime commitment.

She was willing to completely follow God's Word sent through an angel without question or reservation.

William Carey, often called the founder of modern missions, said this: "I'm not afraid of failure; I'm afraid of succeeding at things that don't matter." Mary's decision mattered, and she made the right choice. Doing what God wants is always the right choice.

On each and every day, are you willing to do what God wants you to do? Maybe He wants you to help a needy family, or give an offering to your church, or even volunteer for a ministry.

Amy Carmichael put it this way: "Satan is so much more in earnest than we are--he buys up the opportunity while we are wondering how much it will cost."

Where God guides He will always supply. This next Christmas, let's listen to the Word of God and make a difference in the things which truly matter.

"Ye are the salt of the earth: but if the salt have lost his savour, wherewith shall it be salted? it is thenceforth good for nothing, but to be cast out, and to be trodden under foot of men." Matthew 5:13

Lions Are Not Pets

A pet lion mauled to death a Czechoslovakian man a while back. Repeatedly this man was denied permission to own a lion but he ignored the warnings and the law. Sadly, the 33-year-old paid dearly for his negligence.

Most readers would never have a lion, and don't want to see one anywhere but the zoo. So, what can we learn from this unfortunate story that we can apply to our lives?

The Bible says tells us in I Peter 1:8: "Be sober, be vigilant; because your adversary the devil, as a roaring lion, walketh about, seeking whom he may devour."

J. Hand said, "You know the lion is dangerous when it is quiet, stalking, sneaking up on its prey. Only after it has ambushed and killed its prey does the lion roar."

Satan is not someone to play with. He wants to destroy everything good in your life. Even Michael the archangel did not want to deal with the Devil (Jude 1:9). Unfortunately, many people do not fear this "lion" like they should.

This lion devours marriages and homes. This lion lures people into his trap. Drugs, drinking, and pornography are just a few of the snares that he sets. Destroyed lives are a regular occurrence for this lion. Do not think that you can keep him for a pet. He cannot be controlled.

II Corinthians 2:11 challenges, "Lest Satan should get an advantage of us: for we are not ignorant of his devices." When you know what is coming you are better prepared to deal with the problem. You know that a lion is strong and unpredictable. You know he has powerful jaws and razor-sharp claws. You know he is a predator.

Acts 26:18 says, "To open their eyes, and to turn them from darkness to light, and from the power of Satan unto God." God can put the lion back in the fence where he belongs. Let God rule your life, not the Devil.

It Is Well with My Soul

A few years ago, this pastor had the opportunity to visit the grave of Horatio Spafford. Spafford penned the words to the famous hymn "It Is Well with My Soul". He is buried in Jerusalem in Mount Zion Cemetery. It is a private cemetery that tourists rarely get to see, and it was a blessing to have this unforgettable opportunity.

The hymn was written after a series of painful events in Spafford's life. The first two were the death of his four-year-old son and the Great Chicago Fire of 1871, which devastated him financially. His business interests were further hit by the economic downturn of 1873, at which time he had planned to travel to Europe with his family on the ship *SS Ville du Havre*.

In a late change of plan, he sent the family ahead while he was delayed on business concerning zoning problems following the Great Chicago Fire.

While crossing the Atlantic, the vessel sank rapidly after a collision with another ship, killing all four of Spafford's daughters. His wife Anna survived and sent him the sad telegram, "Saved alone ..."

Shortly afterwards, as Spafford traveled to meet his grieving wife, he was stirred to write the now renowned hymn as his ship passed near where his daughters had perished.

> When peace like a river, attendeth my way,
> When sorrows like sea billows roll;
> Whatever my lot, Thou hast taught me to know
> It is well, it is well, with my soul.
>
> It is well, (it is well),
> With my soul, (with my soul)
> It is well, it is well, with my soul.
>
> Though Satan should buffet, though trials should come,
> Let this blest assurance control,
> That Christ has regarded my helpless estate,
> And hath shed His own blood for my soul.
>
> My sin, oh, the bliss of this glorious thought!
> My sin, not in part but the whole,

Is nailed to the cross, and I bear it no more,
Praise the Lord, praise the Lord, O my soul!

The Psalmist wrote, "He hath delivered my soul in peace from the battle that was against me: for there were many with me." No matter the trials you face, you can get through them if your soul is well. Knowing Christ as your personal Savior is the greatest peace that a human can know this side of eternity.

1 Peter 5:7 says, "Casting all your care upon him; for he careth for you."

And Lord, haste the day when my faith shall be sight,
The clouds be rolled back as a scroll;
The trump shall resound, and the Lord shall descend,
Even so, it is well with my soul.

It is well, (it is well),
With my soul, (with my soul)
It is well, it is well, with my soul.

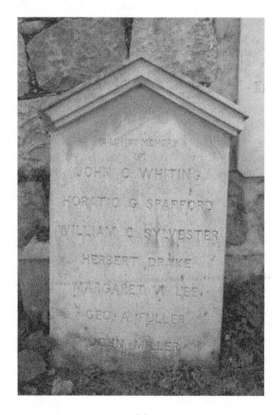

Promotion of Praise

Psalm 150 is the concluding chapter of a book of praise. Whether it is a Psalm 1 challenge on serving God, or a Psalm 23 challenge on simple faith, or a Psalm 100 challenge on serious praise, the book of Psalms speaks volumes on the power of praising God in our lives.

King David summarizes the preceding 149 chapters in a memorable conclusion in chapter 150. David knew the value of praising God: he praised God as a young man with the sheep, as a soldier on the battlefield, and as a king on the throne. We can learn from him some valuable truths about praising God.

We see in verse one that the place of praise is in the sanctuary. God's house is the center of praise for a Christian. Take time out every week to faithfully take part in your church and fervently praise God. We praise him in our singing, in our service, and in our sacrificial giving. God's house is a refuge from the world and a house of praise to our Master.

We see that the Person of praise is God. Ps 86:12, "I will praise thee, O Lord my God, with all my heart: and I will glorify thy name for evermore." God and God alone is worthy of our unrestrained praise.

This chapter gives us the pattern of praise. There are many tools listed here to praise God with, but this is not a completed list. God wants us to use the tools of our life to praise Him, and God wants our life to pattern for others this idea of praise. Could others pattern their praise after you and be a person of praise? A lack of praise in our lives takes away the attention from Him and unfortunately that attention often directs inwardly, and that is not a good thing.

Are we promoters of praise? Verse 6 says, "Let everything that hath breath praise the Lord." Are you breathing this morning? Then you are a vessel of praise. Psalm 29:2, "Give unto the Lord the glory due unto his name; worship the Lord in the beauty of holiness." We cannot praise God too much! We cannot promote God too much! We cannot pursue God too much! Our praise can and will make a difference! Psalm 40:3, "And he hath put a new song in my mouth, even praise unto our God: many shall see it, and fear, and shall trust in the Lord."

Facing Fear Fearlessly

"He who fears he will suffer, already suffers because he fears." Fear is overwhelming our society. People have reasons to be afraid as violence is common, storms are brewing, and viruses are invasive. Fear has even reached its tentacles into the church and caused such fear that many are no longer regular in their worship. Church doors are even closed temporarily and sometimes permanently.

As a believer, how should we live in a time like this? 2 Timothy 1:7 says, "For God hath not given us the spirit of fear; but of power, and of love, and of a sound mind." As a Christian, we should not be "shaking in our boots" over what is happening in our world. Psalm 118:6 says, "The LORD is on my side; I will not fear: what can man do unto me?"

When thinking of fear, it reminds this pastor of 2 Kings chapter 6. The prophet Elisha and his servant are surrounded by the enemy during the night. The servant gets up early and discovers what has happened. He is very afraid and says, "Master, what shall we do?"

Elisha is unconcerned. He says, "Fear not: for they that be with us are more than they that be with them." Elisha had spiritual insight to see things that others did not see. He walked with God and understood His power.

We need the spirit of Elisha today! Is it gone? I surely hope not. Hebrews 13:6 says, "So that we may boldly say, The Lord is my helper, and I will not fear what man shall do unto me."

Our world is desperate to see some real bravery, and who better to display it than the Christian? Someone said this: "Let us not pray to be sheltered from dangers but to be fearless when facing them."

"Faith looks not at what happens to him but at Him
Whom he believes." — Watchman Nee

"How sweet the name of Jesus sounds, in a believer's
ear! It soothes his sorrows, heals his wounds, and
drives away his fear." — John Newton

"But even the very hairs of your head are all numbered. Fear not
therefore: ye are of more value than many sparrows." Luke 12:7

Almost Persuaded

"Almost only counts in horseshoes and hand grenades." This has been a common phrase when someone "almost" gets something done. Nuclear bombs could be added to this list, but you get the picture.

In Acts 26, the Apostle Paul delivers a passionate sermon to some important men. One of those men had his heart stirred by the message, but that was as far as it went. King Agrippa says to Paul at the close of the sermon, "Almost thou persuadest me to be a Christian."

Just hearing the message and having an earnest answer only qualifies as an "almost". Mark Twain said, "The difference between the right word and the almost right word is the difference between lightning and the lightning bug." King Agrippa's words ultimately feel empty and shallow.

John 3:3 says, "Jesus answered and said unto him, Verily, verily, I say unto thee, Except a man be born again, he cannot see the kingdom of God." Accepting the gospel message is simply the only way to Heaven.

There could be some reading this that are similar to King Agrippa. They have heard the message, and it touched their heart. They have almost accepted the truth, but at the last moment they turned away.

Matthew 7:22-23 tells us, "Many will say to me in that day, Lord, Lord, have we not prophesied in thy name? and in thy name have cast out devils? and in thy name done many wonderful works? And then will I profess unto them, I never knew you: depart from me, ye that work iniquity."

Someday everyone will stand before the Lord and give an account. In that day, almost will not work! Do not wait another day. "Behold, now is the accepted time; behold, now is the day of salvation."

"Almost persuaded to be a Christian is like the man who was almost pardoned, but he was hanged; like the man who was almost rescued, but he was burned in the house. A man that is almost saved is damned." -- Charles Hadden Spurgeon

Time Travel

If you could travel back in time, what would you do differently? How far would you go back?

If you are a history buff, maybe you would return to a favorite spot in time. If you have made a poor choice in life, or had a disaster strike, you might return to just before that moment so you could fix your mistakes.

This is fun to think about, but rather pointless. We all know that the only direction in time we can go is forward. Job asked, "Is there not an appointed time to man upon earth?" (Job 7:1)

The answer is yes — we all have an appointed number of hours, days, weeks, months, and years. Paul wrote in I Corinthians 7:29, "But this I say, brethren, the time is short."

This pastor played and coached college basketball, and in each game, there was offered to each team several timeouts. During these the time clock would not move. Sometimes we wish that we could just have a timeout to stop the clock of time, but this cannot be done. Our allotted time moves on whether we like it or not.

All we can do is redeem the time (Ephesians 5:16). James 4:14 says, "Whereas ye know not what shall be on the morrow. For what is your life? It is even a vapour, that appeareth for a little time, and then vanisheth away."

One day, we will close our eyes in death, and time will no longer matter to us. Are you ready for that day?

Romans 13:11 says, "And that, knowing the time, that now it is high time to awake out of sleep: for now is our salvation nearer than when we believed."

Psalm 37:39 says, "But the salvation of the righteous is of the LORD: he is their strength in the time of trouble."

"God has set Eternity in our heart, and man's infinite capacity cannot be filled or satisfied with the things of time and sense." F.B. Meyer

The Judge Gives Grace

God's grace is free. Not much is truly free these days, and many things advertising such have hidden costs attached. Grace is totally free to us, but it does have a cost for Someone. Jesus Christ paid a hefty price of our sin. He laid down His life as payment, making it possible for us to receive the grace of God.

There is only one explanation for such a sacrifice — love. John 3:16 tells us, "For God so loved the world, that he gave his only begotten Son, that whosoever believeth in him should not perish, but have everlasting life."

Years ago, Billy Graham was traveling through a small town in the south, and a police officer pulled him over for excessive speeds. Graham immediately admitted his guilt, but the lawman insisted that he had to appear in court that day. At the court hearing, the judge asked the famous question, "Guilty, or not guilty?" Graham pleaded guilty, and the judge gave the verdict, "That will be ten dollars — one dollar for every mile you were going over the speed limit."

About this time, the judge recognized the famous preacher. "You have violated the law," he said. "The fine must be paid, but I am going to pay it for you." The judge took ten dollars out of his own pocket and paid the fine, and then took Graham out and bought him a steak dinner.

That act of grace pictures how God treats us when we are willing to repent. Christ died so that we could go free. He became a willing sacrifice so we could receive His grace.

John 3:17 says, "For God sent not his Son into the world to condemn the world; but that the world through him might be saved." Have you accepted this gift of grace?

"The future is as bright as the promises of God." — William Carey

"I am not what I ought to be. I am not what I want to be. I am not what I hope to be. But still, I am not what I used to be. And by the grace of God, I am what I am." — John Newton

Courageous Commitment

Proverbs 16:3 says, "Commit thy works unto the LORD, and thy thoughts shall be established."

We live in a day of no commitment. People are no longer committed to marriage, church, and the company they work for. Folks make purchases of homes and cars without a sense of moral obligation to make the payments. Athletes sign contracts one day and break the same contract the next. Even the phone and internet companies are offering no commitment plans to cater to a society that prefers that very thing.

In 1519, the Spanish explorer, Cortez, landed in Vera Cruz, Mexico. His purpose in coming was to conquer the area with a small force of 700 men. When all the men and supplies were ashore, Cortez ordered the ships burned. The small army watched from the shore as their only means of retreat burned and sank in the Gulf of Mexico. Forward into the Mexican interior was the only direction left to go. Retreat was no longer an option.

Commitment requires courage. The Bible story of Daniel is a great example. In Daniel 1:8 it tells us, "But Daniel purposed in his heart that he would not defile himself..." Daniel decided early on that He was going to commit to the cause, and years later he was able to face the lion's den with courage because of that decision.

The apostle Paul stayed committed to the end, and he wrote in his last recorded book, "I have fought a good fight, I have finished my course, I have kept the faith." If you want to finish like Paul than you need to commit your life as he did.

Why not make a new commitment to the Lord today? The years before us require courage. Like Cortez, you may need to "burn some bridges" and keep pressing forward.

"In all true faith there is complete committal
to God." — Lee Roberson

Why So Much Pain?

The prophet asked God this question in Jeremiah 15:18: "Why is my pain perpetual, and my wound incurable, which refuseth to be healed?" Perpetual has the idea of a strong, everlasting pain. This is both a mental and physical agony that cannot be wiped away with a quick trip to the doctor or a pharmaceutical prescription.

Job suffered from this overwhelming pain, and his friends noticed. Job 2:13 says, "So they {his friends} sat down with him {Job} upon the ground seven days and seven nights, and none spake a word unto him: for they saw that his grief was very great."

Why is there so much hurting in this world? I do not think that this question is answered completely in this short piece, but there are answers found in the Scriptures. Jeremiah received an immediate answer. In Jeremiah 15:20, God says, "I will make thee unto this people a fenced brasen wall: and they shall fight against thee, but they shall not prevail against thee: for I am with thee to save thee and to deliver thee, saith the LORD."

"Brasen" is hardened and tempered, like steel. God will make you strong enough to handle what comes your way. God knows the end from the beginning, and He can make us strong enough to withstand anything this world sends our direction.

God continued in verse 21 by saying, "I will deliver thee out of the hand of the wicked, and I will redeem thee out of the hand of the terrible."

The Lord does not promise we will not have troubles but promises to deliver the righteous in time of trouble. Pain is going to come our way, but deliverance is available to those who trust in Him.

Jesus understands great pain, even perpetual pain. He suffered as no one ever has on the cross for our sins. 1 Peter 2:21 says, "For even hereunto were ye called: because Christ also suffered for us, leaving us an example, that ye should follow his steps."

If you are suffering mental or physical distress, turn to the Great Physician. He understands your pain more than you do yourself.

I Want to Be Appreciated

Do you ever feel your service is not appreciated? You are not the only person. An elderly missionary was returning home after many years of service. He and his wife had given their best years serving in Africa. He buried his wife and two children in the jungle. He had sacrificed more than most and was sick and weary.

As he exited the airplane, he saw many people holding banners and signs waiting at the gate. For a few moments he thought, "Can it be? After more than forty years of service, these people have actually come out to welcome me home?"

It was not for him. On the same plane was a famous official returning from a visit to Africa. While in Africa and traveling this man had every whim and need met. He returned home like a conquering hero.

Not a person showed up to welcome the old missionary. As he watched the festivities for the famous official, the man's sadness became almost unbearable. Tears came, and he began to feel sorry for himself.

After a while, the missionary started to pray. "Lord God in Heaven, why? I've served You faithfully for so long. I don't assume much. Is it wrong to wish for there be some kind of a welcome home?" In his heart, the old man heard the Lord say, "My child, you are not home yet." Wow, what a truth!

Jesus said to His disciples, "In my Father's house are many mansions. I go to prepare a place for you." Jesus then continued, "I will come again, and receive you unto myself; that where I am, there ye may be also." Please stay faithful. Your service has caught heaven's attention and reward will come in due time. You are not home yet.

"Yes, give thanks for "all things" for, as it has been well said, "Our disappointments are but His appointments." -- A.W. Pink

"You say, 'If I had a little more, I should be very satisfied.' You make a mistake. If you are not content with what you have, you would not be satisfied if it were doubled." -- Charles H. Spurgeon

What Really Makes America Great

"Make America Great Again" is part of our modern political discourse, but what is greatness?

Lots of people have ideas on how to make America great. Some feel unions make national greatness. Others believe libraries and reading make our country great. Some think immigration makes America great, and many consider wealth as true greatness. Texans mostly agree that Texas itself makes America great!

What does the Bible say about greatness? Matthew 22:37-39 says, "Thou shalt love the Lord thy God with all thy heart, and with all thy soul, and with all thy mind. This is the first and great commandment. And the second is like unto it, Thou shalt love thy neighbor as thyself."

From the words of Jesus, here is what makes us great. Loving the Word of God, the Lord, and others is the three-fold key to greatness. We live in a generation that despises commandments, but these are commandments that will change lives for the better.

Jesus said in John 14:15, "If ye love me, keep my commandments." We are to love the Lord with all our heart, with all our soul, and with all our mind. Jesus continues by telling us that just as we love Him, we are to love our neighbors.

We know who our neighbor is from the story of the Good Samaritan. A Jewish man was assisted by a Samaritan while other Jews walked right past his needs. Following this humble example would solve much of our racial tension and make us great again.

Mark 12:33 says, "And to love him with all the heart, and with all the understanding, and with all the soul, and with all the strength, and to love his neighbor as himself, is more than all whole burnt offerings and sacrifices." Simply stated, it is better to love Christ and your neighbor than to give an offering, to do church work, or impress the elders.

Let's make America great again by following this simple formula for greatness.

The Miracle of Freedom

It would have been impossible for America to have won the Revolutionary War and freedom without God's help. It was a 'David vs. Goliath' battle, and Goliath wins every time unless God intervenes. Seven years before he died, George Washington wrote, "I am sure that never was there a people who had more reason to acknowledge a Divine interposition in their affairs, than those of the United States."

One of the amazing battles early in the war was the battle of Bunker Hill, which was actually fought on Breeds Hill. Why does history still name it to have been fought on Bunker Hill? I believe it was because the spiritual battle was fought there by a Connecticut Baptist preacher named David Avery. Avery wrote in his diary, "I stood on a neighboring hill (Bunker) with hands uplifted, supplicating the blessing of Heaven to crown our unworthy arms with success…" As he prayed, historians write that one could literally feel the surge of reassurance pervade the ranks below him. Many feel that the bitter experience at this battle psychologically crippled the British for the remainder of the war. General Gage wrote, "The success, which was very necessary in our present condition, cost dear." There is no doubt that they showed a healthy respect for American forces after this bloody battle. The British "won" this battle at great cost, but the real victory was won by a chaplain on the higher elevation who prayed during the entire conflict.

If space would allow, many more miracles could be shared of God's power to give us freedom. It is sad to watch as America turns away from the One Who created her. I challenge you to recognize the God who gave you this freedom by attending church this weekend and to thank Him for the freedoms you have enjoyed. My prayer is that God will continue to show mercy on this nation.

"May we think of freedom, not as the right to do as we please, but as the opportunity to do what is right." — Peter Marshall

A Pastor's Perspective of 9/11

Jesus said in Matthew 5:4, "Blessed are they that mourn: for they shall be comforted."

It has been over 20 years since that fateful day that changed our lives so dramatically. We all remember where we were on 9-11-01. I had just graduated from seminary in Greenwood, Indiana and was on staff at the university as a teacher and athletic director. I remember the college president flagging my car down as I drove across campus to tell me the news.

We set up televisions in the common areas, and student and teacher alike glued themselves to them throughout the day. There was anger about what had happened, and fear that it could happen again. Most had never heard of the al-Qaeda until that day, but we have never forgotten that name since.

I remember the patriotism that followed that event. People gave blood that have never given blood. We all waved flags. Our common cause galvanized us together.

George W. Bush said, "Time is passing. Yet, for the United States of America, there will be no forgetting September the 11th. We will remember every rescuer who died in honor. We will remember every family that lives in grief. We will remember the fire and ash, the last phone calls, the funerals of the children."

I have been to Ground Zero and prayed for the families of those that have lost their lives. It is a solemn feeling to stand at the very place where everything transpired.

As tragic as 9/11 was, it was something that brought us back to God as a nation. I do not wish for another tragedy, but I do wish that our nation would turn back to the Lord. Psalm 33:12 says, "Blessed is the nation whose God is the LORD…"

Twenty years have passed very rapidly. James 4:14 says, "Whereas ye know not what shall be on the morrow. For what is your life? It is even a vapour, that appeareth for a little time, and then vanisheth away." Are you prepared for eternity? Acts 2:21 says, "…whosoever shall call on the name of the Lord shall be saved."

The Church and Racism

Racism is a heated issue today, and sadly most of the world has chosen an unpleasant response to the issue. Jeremiah 13:23 says, "Can the Ethiopian change his skin, or the leopard his spots? then may ye also do good, that are accustomed to do evil."

Although it is not the primary emphasis, this verse clearly shows the folly of racism. No one can change their skin. It is a gift from God. People cannot affect their color and they should not want to do so.

God is not color blind, since He made people red, yellow, black, white and brown after His own image. We should all be glad just the way that God created us.

Racism has been around for a long time. Numbers 12:1 says, "And Miriam and Aaron spake against Moses because of the Ethiopian woman whom he had married." God brought judgment into their lives because of this. God is not a respecter of persons, and neither should anyone else be.

As a white man, this pastor believes that most in the Christian white community care about black people and are horrified at the tragic injustices in our nation. The white community cares about other ethnic groups as well. Sadly, our predominately white churches have often spoken in hushed tones or merely remained quiet on this subject.

Today, we know more than any previous generation. We have access to more information. The church simply knows better. James 4:17 warns us, "Therefore to him that knoweth to do good, and doeth it not, to him it is sin."

Now that we know better, we owe it to ourselves to do better. 2 Thessalonians 3:5 says, "And the Lord direct your hearts into the love of God, and into the patient waiting for Christ."

The God in whose likeness we are all made calls us to that higher place of loving people as we love ourselves. The church must lead the way and not be struggling to keep up.

The Little Engine That Could

Most of us have heard of the story of "The Little Engine That Could". The moral of the story was to teach children the value of confidence.

The "little engine" was the only one who was willing to pull the train over the tall mountain. All the other engines were either too new and proud or too old and rusty, but they all made fun of the little engine. The little engine just said, "I think I can, I think I can." Finally, the little engine made it over the top and down the other side. "I thought I could, I thought I could," rejoiced the little engine.

Almost everyone admires this trait, so what is a biblical perspective of confidence? We often find secular confidence in wealth, skill or ability, but a spiritual view of confidence comes from a difference source. That source is God himself.

Jesus said in Mark 10:27, "With men it is impossible, but not with God: for with God all things are possible." In Numbers 13, the ten spies returned with a description of the land of Canaan. The report was that the place was amazing but the people unbeatable and the Israelites should give up and turn back. Caleb, one of the spies, disagreed: "Let us go up at once, and possess it." Do you think Caleb was cocky and brash? No, because the Lord had said that the land was theirs, and he simply believed God. Do you believe God?

God-confidence is a mighty weapon when used in our lives. It will overcome depression, doubt, and defeat if we will let it. For the Christian, our battle cry is this: "I know He can, I know He can." When we win victories, we then say, "I knew He could, I knew He could!"

God Cares for Sparrows.

Many folks enjoy bird watching. One of my daughters put out a hummingbird feeder for a school project, and what joy she had to see them hover in to drink. It was cute to watch her sit at the window watching those little birds fly around. Her enthusiasm about the venture was contagious, and often other siblings would be lined up peering out the window in hopes of seeing another one come by.

Did you know that God is a bird watcher? Jesus spoke in Matthew 10:29, "Are not two sparrows sold for a farthing? and one of them shall not fall on the ground without your Father {knowing}." A farthing was a Roman coin equal to a half penny of our money. Jesus was saying that a sparrow is not worth much, but God cares so much about little birds that He notices every time one is in distress.

Jesus goes on to say in Matthew 10:31, "Fear ye not therefore, ye are of more value than many sparrows." The comparison Christ was making was that if He cares about a little bird (which he does), then just think how much more He care about us. Just considering that fact should take a big load off of our soul. I Peter 5:7 encourages us with this thought, "Casting all your care upon him; for he careth for you."

East Texas is home to some of the prettiest birds in the world. Many of you regularly feed these little guests at feeders in your yards or on your porches. The next time you are bird watching, remember God is watching as well. That should remind us that He is watching us with even greater loving care.

"The safest place in all the world is in the will of God, and the safest protection in all the world is the name of God." -- Warren Wiersbe

"When thou passest through the waters, I *will be* with thee; and through the rivers, they shall not overflow thee: when thou walkest through the fire, thou shalt not be burned; neither shall the flame kindle upon thee." Isaiah 43:2

What Are You Thinking?

This question is often raised in a frustrated tone to one of our six children. What are you thinking? It is a rhetorical question because there has been little thinking going on, which has led to the problem.

This query is a good one to ask ourselves. What is on our mind? Proverbs 23:7a says, "For as he thinketh in his heart, so is he...". Our thoughts are important to God and will shape our future actions.

Have you found it difficult to control your thoughts during these days? This writer has. Every visit to social media is like a roller coaster of emotions and thoughts. Covid-19 has affected our thinking on every level. What can we do about it?

Philippians 4:8 says, "Finally, brethren, whatsoever things are true, whatsoever things are honest, whatsoever things are just, whatsoever things are pure, whatsoever things are lovely, whatsoever things are of good report; if there be any virtue, and if there be any praise, think on these things."

Apostle Paul wrote this while sitting in a Roman prison cell, so we know the author was an expert on problems. Even in such a situation, Paul was able to write with confidence about controlling the mind.

The challenge is to focus on truthfulness, purity, and virtue. It would be easy to get depressed in a dirty cell, but Paul kept his mind on good things. There are lots of good things for us to direct our attention toward during our "trial" as well. I Peter 1:7 says, "That the trial of your faith, being much more precious than of gold that perisheth, though it be tried with fire, might be found unto praise and honour and glory at the appearing of Jesus Christ."

What has your focus this week? Are your thoughts directed toward things you cannot control? Someone said this: "If you're in a bad mood, take a deep breath. If you're in a good mood, give thanks to God."

Someone is Watching

1 Thessalonians 1:3 says, "Remembering without ceasing your work of faith, and labour of love, and patience of hope in our Lord Jesus Christ, in the sight of God and our Father;"

You are being watched. There is someone watching everything you do. There is no place you can go without being seen. In a town the size of Jefferson, our citizens understand this better than most. This pastor almost never leaves the house without seeing people that I know. What is it that people are watching?

They are watching our faith. They are watching to see if your life matches up to what your mouth says. If you say you are a Christian, you can be sure that people are watching to see if you are the real deal. You may feel like nobody sees what you are doing for the Lord, but people are watching.

They are also watching your love. You say that you love, so people watch to see if you really mean it. They see you give the money to those in need. They see you at the hospital in their hour of need. They see your concern when they are hurting. You may think that you are loving in vain, but your love is being watched.

They are also watching your patience. They see you continually work with those that seem undeserving. They see you repeatedly help someone who has failed over and over again because you believe eventually they will turn their life around. Though you may at times feel that nobody really understands what you do, let me remind you that you are being watched.

God is always watching. Other Christians in your church or fellowship are often watching. Your community is watching. Remember, someone sees what you do and they may be encouraged to keep going by your faithfulness. Proverbs 20:6 says, "Most men will proclaim every one his own goodness: but a faithful man who can find?"

What the Bible says about Wearing Masks

Today, you can go to Wal Mart and see more people wearing a mask than one used to see at the hospital. Since antiquity, masks have been available for protection, so there is nothing wrong with using one for that reason. People are wearing masks for their safety and the safety of others.

With all the hype about wearing a mask, I decided to go to the Bible and see what it says about mask wearing. It proved an interesting study.

The first Bible mention of a face covering is in Genesis 24:65: "For she had said unto the servant, What man is this that walketh in the field to meet us? And the servant had said, It is my master: therefore she took a vail, and covered herself." If you have ever been to the Middle East or attended a wedding, you understand what Rebekah was doing here.

In Exodus 34:33, Moses had been in the presence of the Lord, and his face was shining so bright it was terrifying the people. He had to use a face covering so that they would not run from him. Some have suggested that this writer do the same because my face scares them!

In Isaiah 6:2 it tells us about a vision of heaven: "Above it stood the seraphims: each one had six wings; with twain he covered his face, and with twain he covered his feet, and with twain he did fly." These angels are covering their faces with wings.

In the New Testament, it speaks of those that put a mask on their hearts (I Corinthians 3:15). Again, I am not against wearing masks, but there are some things the Bible tells us not to put a mask on.

We should not put a mask on the Scriptures. Spread the Bible far and wide and never "shelter-in" the Truth where no one can hear.

We should never put a mask on our salvation. Hiding salvation is worse than hiding the cure to Covid-19! The Devil hides salvation because he is evil, but a believer should share salvation. In a world using masks to extend and save their physical life, do not mask salvation that can save their spiritual life!

Our Christianity must spiritually unmask even if we mask our natural body. God left us here to shine, and if we do not, who will?

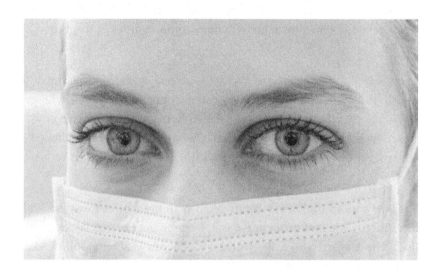

"Let your light so shine before men, that they may see your good works, and glorify your Father which is in heaven." Matthew 5:16

"Ye are the light of the world. A city that is set on an hill cannot be hid." Matthew 5:14

"But ye *are* a chosen generation, a royal priesthood, an holy nation, a peculiar people; that ye should shew forth the praises of him who hath called you out of darkness into his marvellous light." 1 Peter 2:9

"For ye were sometimes darkness, but now *are ye* light in the Lord: walk as children of light." Ephesians 5:8

A Mom Worth Talking About

Phyllis Buckner

Proverbs 31:10 says, "Who can find a virtuous woman? for her price is far above rubies." This pastor has a wonderful mom, and her story is very special to me.

Phyllis Buckner was born in rural Kentucky and grew up very poor. She married young and has been married now for over fifty years. Through much sacrifice, she went to college and graduated. She was a talented educator who had many opportunities in front of her.

Then Seth Buckner was born. With his arrival everything changed for Phyllis. Seth and his younger brother John became her whole world. She quit public work and stayed home to raise her two boys. She homeschooled her two children all twelve grades. She believed her two students could change the world, and she pushed us to excel in everything possible.

She was a mom that never got in touch with the modern way of discipline. One look from her was enough to get her boys back into line. The reason that "look" worked was because of what followed if the "look" was not respected!

Phyllis sacrificed her career to mold the life of her children. Today this writer stands as a testament of her work. Proverbs 31:28 tells us, "Her children arise up, and call her blessed; her husband also, and he praiseth her."

Her greatest attributes were in spiritual things. She taught by example; faithfully attending church, praying, and helping others in need. She sacrificed and did without so that others would have enough. Proverbs 31:20 says, "She stretcheth out her hand to the poor; yea, she reacheth forth her hands to the needy."

Phyllis is truly a Proverbs 31 lady. Proverbs 31:30 says, "Favour is deceitful, and beauty is vain: but a woman that feareth the LORD, she shall be praised."

"My mother was the most beautiful woman I ever saw.
All I am I owe to my mother. I attribute all my success in life
to the moral, intellectual and physical education I received
from her." -- George Washington

"I don't believe there are devils enough in hell to pull a boy
out of the arms of a godly mother." -- Billy Sunday

"Honour thy father and thy mother: that thy days may be long
upon the land which the LORD thy God giveth thee." Exodus 20:12

"I cannot tell you how much I owe to the solemn word of
my good mother." - Charles Haddon Spurgeon

"Now there stood by the cross of Jesus his mother, and his mother's
sister, Mary the wife of Cleophas, and Mary Magdalene. When
Jesus therefore saw his mother, and the disciple standing by, whom
he loved, he saith unto his mother, Woman, behold thy son! Then
saith he to the disciple, Behold thy mother! And from that hour that
disciple took her unto his own home." John 19:25-27

The Influence of a Godly Mother

Proverbs 22:6 says, "Train up a child in the way he should go, And when he is old he will not depart from it." A godly mother can make all the difference for a growing child. Moms, do not take your job lightly.

You are not perfect, but you can do whatever it takes to train your children and bring them up in the ways of the Lord. Your children are watching you and what they see is exactly that they will do. You will influence them one way or another.

The amazing faith of Jochebed, Moses' mother, kept him from being destroyed by a deranged Pharaoh. Her early training shaped his identity as a child of God. She prepared him as a future leader.

Hannah is another great example. She prayed for a child fervently, then gave that child completely to the Lord. Hannah's name means "grace." It is a fitting name for a mom whose life was crowned with grace and who became a living emblem of the grace of motherhood.

Naomi was the mother-in-law to Ruth, but she was a mother figure to her as well. After her husband and sons died, Naomi decided to return to Bethlehem. Her daughter-in-law Ruth followed her. Naomi had taught Ruth enough about God that Ruth wanted to make Naomi's God hers as well.

 Whether you grew up with a godly heritage, a completely dysfunctional one, or don't know what you grew up as, there is always hope. Through Jesus you can have confidence in healing and beginning anew to become a godly mom. Mom, your calling is for such a time as this to make an impact to this generation and the generations to come.

1 Timothy 4:12 says, "Let no man despise thy youth; but be thou an example of the believers, in word, in conversation, in charity, in spirit, in faith, in purity."

Letter to Mom

Dear Mom, I would like to write you and say thank you. We have not always seen eye to eye. In fact, we disagree on many things. You are never afraid to voice your opinion, but you always have good intentions and love in your heart. One thing that we can always agree on is our love for one another.

Mom, I am so grateful for my raising. Proverbs 1:8 says, "My son, hear the instruction of thy father, and forsake not the law of thy mother." I am thankful for the "law" that you set in my life. You were never afraid of your job as a parent -- to put your foot down, to teach me right from wrong, to make sure I did my absolute best. You always let me know I had a mom who cared about me, who believed in me, who was there for me no matter what. Growing up with that kind of love and support made such a difference in my life; it made me who I am today.

As I go through life, I always appreciate your strength and purity, your fierce sense of pride, your generous heart and sensitivity, and your sense of humor. Thank you, Mom, for setting me an example in unconditional devotion to God and your fervent prayer for those around you. Thank you for always believing in me.

Thank you for the many hours rocking me and praying for me as a baby—I think I was a fussy little child! Your prayer was that I would serve God with my life, and I am thankful that God answered those prayers.

Exodus 20:12 says, "Honour thy father and thy mother: that thy days may be long upon the land which the LORD thy God giveth thee." I pray that I will always honor you. I love you with all my heart. With love, your son.

A Father's Importance

Someone wisely said, "Being a father is the most important role I will ever play and if I don't do this well, no other thing I do really matters."

As we think about fathers, it would be a great thing if being a dad could be raised back to its proper importance. Our society seems to revel in dumbing down men in general and fathers in particular.

Television glorifies a world of sissy men that cannot lead to save their lives. Children are portrayed with more wisdom than the father. We probably cannot change Hollywood, but men need to not permit culture to keep them from being a real man.

Men are to be the leaders of the home in spiritual things. Wives and children should allow men to be the spiritual leaders. Dad, your family needs to see you in church. They need to see you reading your Bible and praying. They need to see God in your life, so they will feel the need of God in their own lives. The Bible tells us, "Fathers, provoke not your children to wrath: but bring them up in the nurture and admonition of the Lord."

If your father is living, let him know what he means to you. You would not be here without him. This pastor is thankful for a Dad who took time for him, prayed with him, and guided him. Let your father know that he sincerely affected your life.

Psalm 12:1 says, "Help, LORD; for the godly man ceaseth; for the faithful fail from among the children of men." Let us make this prayer ours on Father's Day. Pray that God would help us see men raised up who would serve the Lord. Pray our churches fill with great fathers. Pray our homes continue to be led by good dads. May the godly man continue forever!

"Train up a child in the way he should go—but be sure you go that way yourself."—Charles Hadden Spurgeon

"I just owe almost everything to my father...it's passionately interesting for me that the things that I learned in a small town, in a very modest home, are just the things that I believe have won the election."—Margaret Thatcher

Think of Others

During these days of living and serving, it is easy to become selfish in our focus. Face-coverings, gloves, and "sheltering in place" could make us begin to think only of our best interest. Of course, safety precautions are a wise step in the day we live, but do not let them make you forget the people around you.

General William Booth lay on his deathbed during the annual conference of the Salvation Army in London. Booth wrote a message on a paper and sent it by messenger to have it read from the podium. Silence fell as the moderator stood before the crowd to read the words. The moderator opened the paper and found just one word written — "others."

This is a reminder of the "Good Samaritan" story in the Bible. The man whom the Samaritan helped had been beaten badly and was probably unknown to him. He was also a Jew, and Jews hated Samaritans. If we could sum up one word to describe this Samaritan it would be — others. He lifted the man on his own donkey, cleaned his wounds, and paid for all the time he needed to recover and get back on his feet.

Philippians 2:4 says, "Look not every man on his own things, but every man also on the things of others." Being caring might take a lot of time, effort and cost, but what a difference maker! Sometimes it may only be a kind word or a listening ear that makes the way better for a hurting neighbor. Listening and loving speaks volumes about how you feel about others.

I Corinthians 13:1 says, "Though I speak with the tongues of men and of angels, and have not charity, I am become as sounding brass, or a tinkling cymbal." This verse simply encourages us to not be "pretty" in our talk but be loving in our walk.

Charles Meigs wrote in 1890: "Others, Lord, yes others; let this my motto be. Help me to live for others, that I may live like Thee. Lord, help me live from day-to-day, in such a self-forgetful way, that even when I kneel to pray, my prayer shall be for – others."

Finding Grace Everywhere

I Peter 5:10 says, "But the God of all grace, who hath called us unto his eternal glory by Christ Jesus, after that ye have suffered a while, make you perfect, stablish, strengthen, settle you."

God's grace is the unmerited favor of God. We do not deserve the grace of God, but it is freely given by Him. God has a reason for everything that happens in your life. He is working on your behalf even when it may seem like He is not. He is working on our behalf even during pandemics.

In the book *The Hiding Place*, Corrie ten Boom tells the story of her imprisonment at Ravensbruck. The barrack they lived in had an epidemic of terrible fleas. Corrie began to complain, but her sister told her they should give thanks for everything. Corrie retorted, "There's no way even God could make me thankful for a flea." As time went on, they realized that their lodging was the only place in the camp that the guards stayed out of simply because of the fleas. Corrie was able to hide the Bible and lead studies with the other prisoners.

Grace is present during the "flea" times of life. Grace brings clarity and reason to a world that says otherwise. "The Solid Rock" was written years ago by a Baptist pastor and is a favorite song of believers everywhere.

> My hope is built on nothing less,
> Than Jesus' blood and righteousness;
> I dare not trust the sweetest frame,
> But wholly lean on Jesus' name.
>
> When darkness veils His lovely face,
> I rest on His unchanging grace;
> In every high and stormy gale,
> My anchor holds within the veil.
>
> On Christ the solid Rock, I stand;
> All other ground is sinking sand,
> All other ground is sinking sand.

How Is Your Joy Count?

The Bible says in James 1:2-3, "My brethren, count it all joy when ye fall into divers temptations; Knowing this, that the trying of your faith worketh patience."

When James uses this word "temptations", he is speaking about difficulties or trials. These are the outside problems that threaten to steal our inside joy. We know trials are definitely going to come.

What are we counting during these days of trials? We can count the days and hope it ends. We can count the people who are having great problems. Or we can do what this verse tells us to do and count the joy.

The word joy means a cheerfulness or calm delight. This does not mean you are jumping up and down over calamity, but you are cheerful, calm and steady through it.

Joy strengthens. There is great strength in putting our life in the hands of the Lord. I John 1:4 says, "And these things write we unto you, that your joy may be full. The Bible will give us strength and is a book that we need during these days. Not Facebook, not the news, but the Bible.

Joy serves. When we are trusting in the Lord, it is easy to serve others. Psalm 100:2 says, "Serve the Lord with gladness..." There are people all around us that need services and help.

Joy surrenders. God surely did not ask my opinion on the trials of my life. It is his will and not mine. Psalm 4:8 says, "I will both lay me down in peace, and sleep: for thou, Lord, only makest me dwell in safety."

Joy stabilizes. In the white-water rapids of the days we live, never have we needed our life stabilized like today. Nahum 1:7 says, "The LORD is good, a strong hold in the day of trouble; and he knoweth them that trust in him." Our community needs to see surrendered and steady Christians during these coming days.

On a scale of one to ten, what is your joy count? We should all aim to get that count up near ten.

Fellowship With God

As Christians, we have no trouble accepting that Jesus is the only way to Heaven. The Bible says in John 14:6, "I am the way, the truth, and the life: no man cometh unto the Father, but by me." What we do have trouble accepting is that the only way to have real fellowship with God is confessing and forsaking our sins.

Psalm 66:18 says, "If I regard iniquity in my heart, the Lord will not hear me." We will not experience a thriving relationship with Jesus if we are living in unconfessed sin.

In parts of Africa they deal with strong Sahara winds that blow clouds of dust in people's homes. In some areas, the residents have to dust their furniture every single day.

In our lives, that dust is an effective picture of sin. Every day we must work on cleaning our lives so that we can have good fellowship with Christ.

Confession is something that should happen every time you sin. Rather than letting sin collect, you should clean quickly, regularly and thoroughly. If you have a bad thought, confess it to God. If you do something that is wrong, confess it to Him.

Confession is one of the awesome privileges of a Christian, and Christ is just a prayer away. God understands our nature, and this is why He gave us I John 1:9: "If we confess our sins, he is faithful and just to forgive us our sins, and to cleanse us from all unrighteousness."

God wants to restore the relationship, so that we can fellowship with Him.

When we sin, we do not stop being the children of God; we simply lose fellowship with Him. Sin affects your communication, but not your eternal destiny. 1 John 1:9 is a life changing verse and we can experience great victory because of its simple promise.

Prayer Is Important

Jesus takes it for granted that believers are going to pray. Matthew 6:5 says, "When thou prayest…" If you believe that prayer is not important, you have not read the Bible enough. We find prayer in the first book of the Bible, the last book of the Bible, and we find prayer today.

God loves constant contact with His children. Prayer should always be real. Luke 18:11-14 says, "The Pharisee stood and prayed thus with himself, God, I thank thee, that I am not as other men are, extortioners, unjust, adulterers, or even as this publican. I fast twice in the week, I give tithes of all that I possess. And the publican, standing afar off, would not lift up so much as his eyes unto heaven, but smote upon his breast, saying, God be merciful to me a sinner. I tell you, this man went down to his house justified rather than the other: for every one that exalteth himself shall be abased; and he that humbleth himself shall be exalted."

A law against prayer did not stop Daniel from praying. When activated, prayer is unstoppable in the believer's life. We should do nothing in any area of life without first taking the time to saturate the matter in prayer. D. L. Moody said, "I'd rather be able to pray than be a great preacher; Jesus Christ never taught His disciples how to preach, but only how to pray."

We can read every book ever written on prayer, but if we never pray it is all in vain. To make prayer truly effective, we must practice prayer. On a scale of 1 – 10, how would you rate your prayer life?

Hudson Taylor said, "The prayer power has never been tried to its full capacity. If we want to see mighty wonders of divine power and grace wrought in the place of weakness, failure and disappointment, let us answer God's standing challenge, 'Call unto me, and I will answer thee, and show thee great and mighty things which thou knowest not!'"

"To be a Christian without prayer is no more possible than to be alive without breathing." - Martin Luther

If You Love Me

So much is said today about loving the Lord, but loving God extends beyond mere verbal assent. We need to realize that love is expressed most clearly in our actions. Men, your wife or girlfriend like to hear that they are loved, but if you never show it, they will cease to believe what they are hearing. The love for God in a Christian will make a child of God do many things for the cause of Christ.

Love for Christ produces faithfulness. I meet many believers who say they love God but rarely show up to worship Him at His house. If I rarely come home to my wife, she is not going to feel like I truly love her, and if I rarely show up at church, the same can be said about my love for Jesus. We should be faithful in our walk for God as well as our witnessing about God. Love produces faithfulness.

Love for Christ produces fellowship. The more love that I have for Jesus Christ, the more I will want to fellowship with Him. Revelation 3:20, "Behold, I stand at the door, and knock: if any man hear my voice, and open the door, I will come in to him, and will sup with him, and he with me." If I fall in love with Jesus, I will also enjoy the company of those that also love Jesus. I John 4:20, "If a man say, I love God, and hateth his brother, he is a liar: for he that loveth not his brother whom he hath seen, how can he love God whom he hath not seen?"

Love for Christ produces fullness in our joy. I know from personal experience that the closer I get to Jesus, the more joyful I become. You cannot draw close to the Man of Peace without experiencing peace! My challenge for this week is not just to talk about our love for God, but to go out and show that love in our walk. Whenever you see a young man or young woman in love, it always affects their actions. They want to be around the one they love all the time. Our world needs some Christians that will so fall in love with Jesus that their actions are changed.

"If loving God with all our heart and soul and might is
the greatest commandment, then it follows that not
loving Him that way is the greatest sin." R. A. Torrey

Famous Lies

Lying is not good, and rarely is not telling the truth justifiable in any situation. The Bible speaks strongly about lying. Proverbs 12:22 says, "Lying lips are abomination to the LORD: but they that deal truly are his delight." Proverbs 21:6 says, "The getting of treasures by a lying tongue is a vanity tossed to and fro of them that seek death."

One of the famous lies in history was the fabrications of Charles Ponzi, who even got the government to name a type of fraud after him. Ponzi was an Italian immigrant in the 1920's who tricked thousands into investing into a postage stamp speculation scheme. At the peak of his scam, he was making $250,000 a day. Each time a new investor paid their money, he would pay off earlier investors to make them believe that they were making profits from a real business. Today we call this kind of fraud a Ponzi Scheme.

Someone said this about honesty; "Honesty is a person's most valuable asset. His or her good name, good reputation, and good word depend on the individual's quality of honesty. A business that operates under the principles of profound honesty is elevated within the community. It is respected and treasured. The absence of honesty is a liability to an individual or business."

Proverbs 12:19 says, "The lip of truth shall be established for ever: but a lying tongue is but for a moment." For Charles Ponzi this was true, and he got caught and charged with 86 counts of mail fraud. Lying and stealing are no way to live, especially for a believer in Christ. Eventually your lies and dishonesty will catch up to you and you will lose your reputation and testimony. Christians, always have determination to tell the truth no matter what.

How Will You Be Remembered?
Elmer Dacus (1927-2020)

On January 14, 2020, one of our church members lost their father, and this pastor traveled to Lindsay, Oklahoma for the funeral service. Elmer Dacus served our country in the United States Army. He served our Lord by teaching Sunday school for over 50 years. He served his wife and stayed married to the same lady for 69 years. He served his generation by being a man of the Bible who taught his family to serve the Lord.

During the funeral service, it became very evident that this was a special man. It was not hard to tell. From the packed church house, the words of the speakers and singers, and the heart of the family. Tears were shed but there was also laughter and joy in the knowledge of Heaven.

At every funeral, we are reminded that life is short. James 4:14 says, "Whereas ye know not what shall be on the morrow. For what is your life? It is even a vapour, that appeareth for a little time, and then vanisheth away."

If we were to die today, how would we be remembered? Would we be remembered fondly and lovingly, or would we invoke a different spirit? Matthew 12:35 says, "A good man out of the good treasure of the heart bringeth forth good things: and an evil man out of the evil treasure bringeth forth evil things." The man who was laid to rest at this funeral was a good man who produced good fruit. He did this because he was a follower of Christ.

Don't Worry

The Bible says in Proverbs 27:1, "Boast not thyself of tomorrow; for thou knowest not what a day may bring forth."

Many years ago, a group of travelers traveled west during the early spring. In this group was an elderly minister who had made this trip before.

Because of torrential rains, many of the creeks and waterways they encountered were flooded and difficult to cross. As they made another rainy camp one night, they began discussing a large river that they expected to come to the next day. Most in the group did not think they would be able to cross safely.

Finally, after much discussion, they asked the minister what he thought. "Well, gentlemen," said the preacher, "I have learned never to cross a river until I reach it." With that statement, he headed for his bedroll and fell asleep.

There is a Bible verse that goes along with this wise man's statement. Matthew 6:34 says, "Take therefore no thought for the morrow: for the morrow shall take thought for the things of itself. Sufficient unto the day is the evil thereof."

The Bible is telling us not to waste time being anxious about things that we cannot control. Each day brings with it cares enough on its own. The future is in God's hands and needless worry about tomorrow only makes us miserable today. Someone put it this way; "Worrying is like a rocking chair, it gives you something to do, but it doesn't get you anywhere."

What problem are you worrying about? I Peter 5:7 encourages us, "Casting all your care upon him; for he careth for you." Take a few minutes to pray about the situations in your life and ask the Lord to help you with your worry. Trust Him to take care of you.

"Worry is nothing but practical infidelity. The person who worries reveals his lack of trust in God and that he is trusting too much in self." — Lee Roberson

Do You Have a Leak?

Actor Spencer Tracy said, "Acting is not an important job in the scheme of things. Plumbing is." Having a water leak in your plumbing system is not fun, especially if it cannot be located easily.

Water follows the path of least resistance and where you see water surface is often not where the problem is. Experts in the field cannot always locate what is going on, but a leak must be fixed or much damage will probably occur over time.

There is a similarity in the Christian's life. Many problems can occur out of sight without a simple answer or fix. The surface problem is usually just a symptom of a greater problem that is deeper and more complex. Experts, pastors, and psychologist often cannot seem to help. The problem usually must be fixed or damage will be great both physically and emotionally. King David cried out, "Plead my cause, and deliver me: quicken me according to thy word."

Thankfully, we do have a Guidebook in the Bible and a Master Plumber in God Who has the right answers. Former President Ronald Reagan stated, "Within the covers of the Bible are the answers for all the problems that men face." II Timothy 3:16 says, "All scripture is given by inspiration of God, and is profitable for doctrine, for reproof, for correction, for instruction in righteousness."

Being a plumber is not easy work—that is why they get paid for what they do! Spiritually speaking, when things get out of order below the surface of our lives, call on Jesus and read the Bible, because in them lie an unfailing source of wisdom and comfort for those who seek. Psalm 100 closes with this truth: "For the Lord is good; his mercy is everlasting; and his truth endureth to all generations."

Eat Your Shoe and Keep Your Word!

Can our friends and family trust our words? Those who do business with us should know that we will do exactly what we say. James 5:12 says, "But above all things, my brethren, swear not, neither by heaven, neither by the earth, neither by any other oath: but let your yea be yea; and your nay, nay; lest ye fall into condemnation."

There is a story in the Bible about a man who sold a piece of land to give the money to the Lord but lied about the amount when it came time to give the offering. Ananias and his wife Sapphira both tragically lost their lives because of their deceit. This Bible story teaches the importance of always honoring your word and telling the truth.

Mr. Harlan Hill is a former Trump campaign advisor who promised to eat his shoe if Joe Biden became president but has since reneged on his promise. Hill made the bold promise in an election night party in November of 2020, claiming that he was "one hundred percent" certain of victory for the Republican leader. He stated that if Trump lost "I'll eat my shoe. We'll do it on livestream."

Regardless of your feelings about the election, Mr. Biden is President, and Mr. Hill is a liar if he does not eat that shoe. How could you ever trust him as an advisor? The Bible challenges us in Deuteronomy 23:23, "That which is gone out of thy lips thou shalt keep and perform…"

A Christian should always keep their word in all things. 1 John 2:5 says, "But whoso keepeth his word, in him verily is the love of God perfected: hereby know we that we are in him." Even if the price is high, we should do what we say we will do. In fact, cooked shoe leather is edible to eat (the Donner Party and Native Americans have done it during tough times), so eat your shoe and keep your word!

"Among the things you can give and still keep are
your word, a smile, and a grateful heart." — Zig Ziglar

"Promises are like crying babies in a theater; they should
be carried out at once." — Norman Vincent Peale

Love Is More Than a Day

A few years ago, this pastor was sitting outside of a large grocery store on Valentine's evening near closing time.

Several customers hurriedly exited with balloons and flowers. Even though they waited until the last-minute, they still wanted to show love to a special somebody. Lots of money will be spent this coming week on jewelry, flowers, candy, and high-priced Hallmark cards. Eateries will fill with devoted couples. Some romantics may even "pop the question."

Valentine's Day may be special, but we should not need a calendar to show our love to one another. John 15:12 says, "This is my commandment, that ye love one another, as I have loved you." This is not a once-a-year directive but a daily life challenge. Our love should be greater than a single day or moment.

This season is hard for those who feel unloved or have lost their loved one. The good news is that Jesus Christ cares about that empty place in the human heart.

Jesus took our place on the cross. He bore our sins and He died in our place. Sin has a horrible penalty called death. Jesus paid that penalty for us. What a love story!

Listen to the familiar words of John 3:16. "For God so loved the world, that he gave his only begotten Son, that whosoever believeth in him should not perish, but have everlasting life." This love is life-changing.

Spending money for the one you love is not wrong, but showing care does not always involve money. "I love you" are three words that mean so much but get spoken so rarely. Show someone you love them this week. Tell them you love them. More importantly, communicate God's love to them.

One final message to the men — do not procrastinate until Valentine's night to buy a gift!

Don't Let Your Love Get Cold

This pastor read a story about young woman who was in college. Her boyfriend took her out to a fancy restaurant and gave her roses. When she returned to her dorm, she picked up the campus paper. The newspaper had a section for student messages, and she wanted to see if he had written a sweet message to her. Near the bottom of the page she found it: "Bonnie, what are you looking here for? Aren't dinner and flowers enough? Love, Scott."

There is no reason for our coldness in our love. It will not hurt to show that love in every way possible. In fact, we have every reason to hug those we love a little tighter this year (body heat). A Christian should warm up a room, not cause it to get colder. Matthew's gospel speaks about love in the last days and says that the love of many shall wax cold. Unfortunately, we can see this coldness happening all around us.

The need for the warmth of love is one of our most basic and fundamental needs. Love is powerful because it transforms and grows throughout your life. Do not let your love get cold!

Love is more important than money. Love is greater than power and honor. Let us all decide to love the way a Christian believer should. In Matthew 22:37-40, Jesus shares this great truth: "Thou shalt love the Lord thy God with all thy heart, and with all thy soul, and with all thy mind. This is the first and great commandment. And the second is like unto it, Thou shalt love thy neighbour as thyself. On these two commandments hang all the law and the prophets."

Snow Treasures

Job 28:22a says, "Hast thou entered into the treasures of the snow?"

In the winter of 2021, record snows almost overwhelmed East Texas. Unfortunately, this included covering roads, which limited travel. Many missed work, school, and other events.

Because of these and other problems, it is easy to overlook the treasures of the snow. Our family was dealing with bitter cold, frozen plumbing, power outage possibilities, and even our pontoon boat buried under a collapsed marina.

Instead of focusing on the negative, this writer looked at his own life, and picked out some treasures.

1. A lovely treasure. Not many things are prettier than snow covered trees, and much of our area looks like something from a Hallmark movie. The Psalmist wrote, "Wash me, and I shall be whiter than snow." Enjoy the beauty of this snow while you can.

2. A love treasure. Normally most of this preacher's time is spent in the office, but this week he was "forced" to spend the week at home with his family. It was so much fun sitting around the fireplace playing games and visiting together. This was truly a gem that was more valuable than rubies. Proverbs 15:6a says, "In the house of the righteous is much treasure."

3. A life treasure. Often our society moves at a high rate of speed, but the snow caused us to slow down. Take the time given to recharge for the days ahead. James 4:14 declares, "Whereas ye know not what shall be on the morrow. For what is your life? It is even a vapour, that appeareth for a little time, and then vanisheth away."

4. A Lord treasure. Job 37:6a says, "For he saith to the snow, Be thou on the earth." This snow was sent from God, and that in itself makes it a treasure.

There are other assets of the snow, but those treasures are for you to find during the next snowstorm. Please do not get in such a rush that you miss the wonders and blessings that are all around you. Life is far too short.

God and the Weather

When the "world famous" Punxsutawney Phil saw his shadow on February 2nd, 2021, who could have known Texas was in for a such a cold snap? Although I never put much stock in a groundhog weather report, it does seem like it was pretty accurate this year.

Vesta Kelly said, "Snowflakes are one of nature's most fragile things, but just look what they can do when they stick together." How true that is! Frigid temperatures broke records in Texas, but thankfully the unusual cold eventually moved out of our area.

In a day when much credit is given to climate change, what forces really govern the elements? If you believe the Bible, you understand that God ultimately controls the weather. Nahum 1:3 says, "The LORD hath his way in the whirlwind and in the storm, and the clouds are the dust of his feet."

God sent a destructive flood in Noah's day but withheld the rain for three years in Elijah's time. He sent darkness to the Egyptians and light to the Hebrews. God sent wind to part the Red Sea so His people could cross and escape. Jesus calmed the wind with His voice after walking on the water, bringing peace to his frightened disciples.

Matthew 5:45 tells us that God sends "rain on the just and on the unjust." Not all storms are judgment, but God does use weather to get people's attention. Psalm 148:8 says, "Fire, and hail; snow, and vapor; stormy wind fulfilling his word:"

Our country needs a lesson in trust and awareness of God. Weather often brings us back to the realization that we control very little, but He controls everything. "Trust in the LORD with all thine heart; and lean not unto thine own understanding. In all thy ways acknowledge him, and he shall direct thy paths."

Making a Difference

John F. Kennedy had a timeless quote that is as plain as it is powerful: "One person can make a difference, and everyone should try."

The term "Making a Difference" is used a lot in both secular and Christian circles, but what does it really mean? How can an individual truly be a difference maker?

The word difference is defined as "A point or way in which people or things are not the same." Someone put it this way: "If you desire to make a difference in the world, you must be different from the world."

Today's society encourages similarity to ridiculous levels, and it is easy to get caught up in the "blending in" that the modern church is attempting. This was not God's plan for the Christian or the church. Fear is the driving force that keeps many from difference making decisions.

The Bible is full of stories of difference makers: Noah building the ark, Daniel praying alone, Gideon and his tiny army, Esther standing up for her people, just to name a few. These are people who portray Hebrews 13:6; "So that we may boldly say, The Lord is my helper, and I will not fear what man shall do unto me."

Will we overcome our fear and start changing our future? Simply put, stop imagining the worst and waiting for the perfect time. Not everyone will appreciate your attempts, but some will. Romans 12:1 says, "I beseech you therefore, brethren, by the mercies of God, that ye present your bodies a living sacrifice, holy, acceptable unto God, which is your reasonable service."

Some of the best advice this pastor ever received was from a veteran preacher acquaintance. He said, "Decide where you are going to stand for God, plant a flag in the ground in that place, and let that banner wave. People of all ages and backgrounds will rally to that spot and join you." Psalm 56:3 says, "What time I am afraid, I will trust in thee." Overcome your fear through Jesus and impact the world in these last days.

What is Your Worldview?

A Biblical worldview refers to the basis of ideas and beliefs through which a Christian interprets the world and unites with it. Proverbs 21:12 says, "The righteous man wisely considereth the house of the wicked: but God overthroweth the wicked for their wickedness." Wise Christians will make decisions and choices based on the Bible.

The number one need for a believer is righteousness. The idea in the verse above is of a judge or king who maintains the right. God chose Noah for the ark because of righteous living and destroyed the city of Sodom for the lack of righteousness. Psalm 1:6 says, "For the LORD knoweth the way of the righteous: but the way of the ungodly shall perish." God says that our righteousness is like the great mountains and preserves man and animal alike. He loves righteousness and desires it in His followers.

The number two need is wisdom. The righteous man wisely considers each situation, and makes rational decisions based upon that insight. Proverbs 4:7 says, "Wisdom is the principal thing; therefore get wisdom: and with all thy getting get understanding." Wise decisions will consistently direct the Christian back toward the Bible and holy living.

The number three need to maintain a Christian worldview is consideration. The righteous man wisely considers the house of the wicked. Sensible believers, when they have considered every situation, will not envy the prosperity of evil doers. The temptation is there, but after reflection, they realize the vanity of it all. Psalm 37:16 says, "A little that a righteous man hath is better than the riches of many wicked."

A Biblical worldview will please and honor God. Reflect upon yours this week, and make sure it lines up with Bible principles. A Christian worldview impacts every area of life.

A Golden Sacrifice

Give up desserts? Or cheeseburgers? How about french fries? No problem for the Olympic athletes that are preparing to compete. These men and women consider sacrifices a small price to pay to stand at the top of the podium, hear their national anthem, and have a gold medal placed around their neck. Many athletes have sacrificed time with their family, put in many long hours of training, and do it willingly without complaints.

The Apostle Paul wrote "I beseech you therefore, brethren, by the mercies of God, that ye present your bodies a living sacrifice, holy, acceptable unto God, which is your reasonable service." (Romans 12:1) When asked to do acts of service, Christians often submit a variety of excuses, missing their "golden sacrifice." Paul said that serving God is a "reasonable service." Even our greatest sacrifice is small in comparison to His.

Just as sacrifice and hard work wins Olympic gold, these same traits play an important part in the life of a Christian. The gold medals that we are competing for are not for this side of earth.

Matthew 6:20 says, "But lay up for yourselves treasures in heaven, where neither moth nor rust doth corrupt, and where thieves do not break through nor steal." A Christian should be sacrificing not for the praise of men and women, but to hear God say, "Well done, my good and faithful servant."

Have you considered your "golden sacrifice?" What is it that God has asked you to do for Him? Hebrews 12:1-2, "Wherefore seeing we also are compassed about with so great a cloud of witnesses, let us lay aside every weight, and the sin which doth so easily beset us, and let us run with patience the race that is set before us, Looking unto Jesus the author and finisher of our faith; who for the joy that was set before him endured the cross, despising the shame, and is set down at the right hand of the throne of God."

Celebrate the Timing of God

Sometimes God rearranges our schedules just to prove that His way is better. Romans 11:33 says, "O the depth of the riches both of the wisdom and knowledge of God! How unsearchable are his judgments, and his ways past finding out!"

Several years ago, Heritage Baptist Church had one of the most unique Easter services in the history of the church. God upstaged our special Easter programs with a dramatic storm.

The church served breakfast on Sunday morning and had a great turnout. That was a good thing because only those that came to the breakfast were able to get to the service that day.

At about 10 A.M., a tremendous storm hit the Jefferson area. Heavy rain, high winds, lightning, and hail swept across the church parking lot. At least one car window broke from hail and wind.

The power went out, and the church congregation went into a mad scramble looking for the Christmas candles. At least this was not the year that the pastor stored the candles in the attic and melted down the entire supply!

It was not an option not to have services. It got warm, and the sound system was down, but the service still went forward. This day became one of the most special memories the church has ever had. Nahum 1:3 says, "The LORD hath his way in the whirlwind and in the storm, and the clouds are the dust of his feet."

Spiritual decisions made in that service changed the course of lives. Folks trusted Christ as their personal Savior on this day. Sometimes bad situations turn into a tool for good. The cross is a good example. A. W. Tozer said, "The cross is the lightning rod of grace that short-circuits God's wrath to Christ so that only the light of His love remains for believers."

> "And we know that all things work together for good to them that love God, to them who are the called according to *his* purpose." Romans 8:28

A Worthy Resurrection

What is the value of the resurrection of Jesus? To the Christian, nothing could be more priceless. When Jesus rose from the dead, everything changed. All things in the future were different because of this great event.

Because of this, the resurrection of Christ is worth trusting. This preacher trusts the biblical account with all his heart. This is what faith is all about, but it is a faith well founded and grounded in an infallible Word. Trust in what Jesus did. 1 Peter 1:18-19 says, "Forasmuch as ye know that ye were not redeemed with corruptible things, as silver and gold, from your vain conversation received by tradition from your fathers; But with the precious blood of Christ, as of a lamb without blemish and without spot."

The resurrection is also worth teaching. This message is worth sharing with everyone! The next Easter could be the last Easter Sunday that we experience. Death could take us, or Jesus could return. What are we doing to reach those around us with this great message? The message of the angels shared at the empty tomb was to go quickly and tell others that He arose. Are we doing this great work?

The resurrection is worth trials. Serving God will often bring trials. The Apostle Paul wrote in Philippians 3:10, "That I may know him, and the power of his resurrection, and the fellowship of his sufferings, being made conformable unto his death." Whatever trials come because of our faith in a risen Savior are worth the pain.

The resurrection is worth taking. Today is the day of salvation. Do not wait and continue to put off accepting this free gift. Jesus said, "I am the resurrection, and the life: he that believeth in me, though he were dead, yet shall he live." Romans 6:23 says, "For the wages of sin is death; but the gift of God is eternal life through Jesus Christ our Lord." This is a truth you can know today! 1 John 5:13 says, "These things have I written unto you that believe on the name of the Son of God; that ye may know that ye have eternal life, and that ye may believe on the name of the Son of God."

Making Our Life Count

Someone once said, "A man is not old until regrets take the place of dreams." For the Christian, it may well be put this way, "A man is not old until regrets take the place of the will of God."

As a pastor, I commonly hear the unhappy stories of people who wish they could have another chance at the will of God. They mourn living for self, wealth, business, or pleasure instead of making their life count for God. There is little cheerfulness for squandered days of life.

Nancy Reagan wrote, "You learn something out of everything, and you come to realize more than ever that we're all here for a certain space of time, and, and then it's going to be over, and you better make this count."

In this short window of life, that "appeareth for a little time, and then vanisheth away." What will we accomplish that makes a difference? Only the will of God will truly matter. 1 John 2:17 says, "And the world passeth away, and the lust thereof: but he that doeth the will of God abideth for ever."

It is the will of God that you be saved. 1 John 2:2 says, "And he is the propitiation for our sins: and not for ours only, but also for the sins of the whole world." Jesus Christ died for the whole world, and that includes you. It is His perfect will that you come to Him without delay.

It is the will of God that you live for Him. 1 John 3:17 says, "But whoso hath this world's good, and seeth his brother have need, and shutteth up his bowels of compassion from him, how dwelleth the love of God in him?"

We cannot go back and undo the things of the past, but we can change the future. Live for Jesus with the days you have left. Do His will and serve Him with all your heart. C. T. Studd put it this way: "Only one life,'twill soon be past, only what's done for Christ will last."

Oh, What A Savior!

The hymn "He Hideth My Soul" says, "A wonderful Savior is Jesus my Lord, He taketh my burden away; He holdeth me up and I shall not be moved, He giveth me strength as my day." As we study in the great book of Revelation, we find encouragement in how great Jesus is.

He is a personal Savior. Revelation 1:4 says, "John to the seven churches which are in Asia: Grace be unto you, and peace, from him which is, and which was, and which is to come; and from the seven Spirits which are before his throne." Written to real churches of the author's day, this book still has a particular message for us today.

He is a powerful Savior. Revelation 1:5 says, "And from Jesus Christ, who is the faithful witness, and the first begotten of the dead, and the prince of the kings of the earth. Unto him that loved us, and washed us from our sins in his own blood." His compelling love makes Him the greatest, and His redemption is unequaled in this universe.

He is a promoting Savior. Revelation 1:6 says "And hath made us kings and priests unto God and his Father; to him be glory and dominion for ever and ever. Amen." What a promotion that He has given to those who trust in Him!

He is a persistent Savior. Revelation 1:7 says, "Behold, he cometh with clouds; and every eye shall see him, and they also which pierced him: and all kindreds of the earth shall wail because of him. Even so, Amen." When Jesus decides to come, nothing will hold Him back from returning for His people. As the song says, "What a day that will be, when my Jesus I shall see!"

He is a permanent Savior. Revelation 1:8 says, "I am Alpha and Omega, the beginning and the ending, saith the Lord, which is, and which was, and which is to come, the Almighty." Jesus started it, and He will finish it. Are you on His side?

> "Whatever subject I preach, I do not stop until
> I reach the Savior, the Lord Jesus, for in Him
> are all things." – Charles Hadden Spurgeon

An Example of Friendship

What is a good friend? Well, good friends are loyal and accept you for who you are during both the good and bad times. Good friends are also honest, loyal, and trustworthy. Most importantly, people want friends who listen to them.

In I Samuel 18, Jonathan and David were great friends. They had a strong friendship. The Bible says that their souls were "knit" together. This word meant that they tied themselves together firmly by unbreakable bonds. David wrote in Psalms 133:1, "Behold, how good and how pleasant it is for brethren to dwell together in unity!"

It was a selfless friendship. The Bible says that Jonathan loved David as strongly as he loved himself. That was a wonderful friendship, and one worthy of imitation. Jesus said, "Thou shalt love thy neighbor as thyself."

It was a sacrificial friendship. Jonathan gave David his own robe and his military equipment. Jonathan was the king's son, and this brought great honor to David. A real friend is willing to give in a sacrificial way to help others. Jesus said, "Give to every man that asketh of thee; and of him that taketh away thy goods ask them not again."

It was a steadfast friendship. Jonathan and David made a covenant, or a commitment. These were not just empty words, but a promise of an unwavering friendship. Proverbs 17:17 says, "A friend loveth at all times, and a brother is born for adversity."

What kind of friend are you? Choose your friends carefully, but when you do find a good one, stick with them no matter what. Be the kind of friend that brings those around you closer to God. Remember the great challenge in 1 John 3:16; "Hereby perceive we the love of God, because he laid down his life for us: and we ought to lay down our lives for the brethren."

> "I have friends in overalls whose friendship I
> would not swap for the favor of the kings
> of the world."– Thomas A. Edison

Giant Questions of Faith

When young David met Goliath on the battlefield, he was faced with many questions that challenged his faith. Any battle entered as a Christian will often bring up more questions than answers. That is what faith is all about! Hebrews 11:1 says, "Now faith is the substance of things hoped for, the evidence of things not seen."

David faced frightening questions. Put yourself in the shoes of those within earshot of Goliath. He was a scary dude! David wrote in Psalms, "The LORD is on my side; I will not fear: what can man do unto me?"

David faced family questions. His own brothers thought he was crazy for wanting to take on the giant. Remember, those around you are not always going to react well to faith. Deuteronomy 31:6 says, "Be strong and of a good courage, fear not, nor be afraid of them: for the LORD thy God, he it is that doth go with thee; he will not fail thee, nor forsake thee."

David faced frustrating questions. Goliath was of great size and he took his time making sure that he degraded young David as much as possible. The enemy is always fearful of great faith and will often try to distract anyone who lives that way. Again, David wrote in Psalm 56:4; "In God I will praise his word, in God I have put my trust; I will not fear what flesh can do unto me."

Thankfully, David had a fulfilling question answered. His reward was fitting to the size of his faith. The Bible tells us that God works according to our faith. Noah was probably told that he could not build an ark, but he did. Peter was probably told he could not walk on water, but he did. Faith brings some giant questions but remember that God has all the answers. Who will step out in faith and do something big for God?

"Faith is like radar that sees through the fog -- the reality of things at a distance that the human eye cannot see." - Corrie Ten Boom

"Faith expects from God what is beyond all expectation." - Andrew Murray

A Wise Search

For many years, an archaeologist named Howard Carter searched in vain for the tomb of King Tutankhamen. Most of his peers believed it was a futile search, but Carter disagreed. For more than thirty years he continued his search. Finally, his last sponsor decided to stop funding the project.

In the fall of 1922, with funds almost completely gone, he found a hidden staircase near another tomb. After seemingly endless searching, Carter had located the tomb of King Tut. This would become one of the greatest archaeological finds of all time. Inside the tomb was unfathomable riches which had rested untouched for thousands of years.

Mr. Carter believed that this treasure could be found and put in the years of sacrifice to do it. Even he was not completely certain that this tomb was real — no one really was sure. The application for the Christian comes in our search for the wisdom of God. We can guarantee great reward if we commit to searching for the wisdom of God. It is most certainly real!

Proverbs 2:1-5 says, "My son, if thou wilt receive my words, and hide my commandments with thee; So that thou incline thine ear unto wisdom, and apply thine heart to understanding; Yea, if thou criest after knowledge, and liftest up thy voice for understanding; If thou seekest her as silver, and searchest for her as for hid treasures; Then shalt thou understand the fear of the LORD, and find the knowledge of God."

Do you see the confidence of the promise? If we receive the Word of God, and we seek for it as the treasure that it certainly is, we will without doubt find what we seek. Spend some time this week searching the Bible and you will never walk away disappointed. 2 Timothy 2:15 says, "Study to shew thyself approved unto God, a workman that needeth not to be ashamed, rightly dividing the word of truth."

Is It Good to Walk?

Sadly, Americans do not go walking much anymore. The average American walks around 6,000 steps a day, and in this activity, it pays to be above average.

Walking is a part of healthy living, and doctors are confident that it increases life expectancy. Most of us should walk more.

As good as walking is in the physical realm, it is even better in the spiritual. When we are walking with Christ, that is. Deuteronomy 8:6 says, "Therefore thou shalt keep the commandments of the LORD thy God, to walk in his ways, and to fear him."

If we are going to walk with the Lord, we must go the same direction. Amos 3:3 says, "Can two walk together, except they be agreed?" Walking faithfully with the Lord will increase our understanding of His thoughts and ways.

Walking with the Lord will help in the dark times of life. Use the light of the Word of God to light your path and reinforce your walk with the Lord.

Just as physical walking strengthens the body, spiritual walking will strengthen the soul. How did Daniel get through a terrifying night with the lions? How did the Apostle Paul survive physical and emotional abuse? How did John handle abandonment on a deserted island?

They made it through these difficult days by walking with God before, during, and after their troubles.

If you must choose between physical and spiritual walking, choose the latter. 1 Timothy 4:8a says, "Bodily exercise profiteth little: but godliness is profitable unto all things."

It is great to walk physically and the health benefits are undeniable. Just don't neglect the essentials of spiritual living. Read your Bible today, spend time in prayer, and head to a Bible-believing church this Sunday. Someone said this: "Those who walk with God always reach their destination."

Games People Play

In the 1960's a psychologist wrote a book called *Games People Play* that has sold over five million copies. The author's premise was this: "We think we're relating to other people-- but actually we're all playing games." Psalm 12:2 puts it this way: "They speak vanity everyone with his neighbor: with flattering lips and with a double heart do they speak."

Worse than playing games with each other is when we play games with God. It is a sad testimony when Christians are not honest and upfront in their relationship with the Lord. Christianity should not be something that we turn on at church and turn off in life.

Some believers feel that a religious t-shirt or a cross around their neck means more than it really does. These can be a beautiful display of an inward faith. They can also be just a game. Is your heart right with God, or are you just playing games?

I Samuel 16:7 says, "But the LORD said unto Samuel, Look not on his countenance, or on the height of his stature; because I have refused him: for the LORD seeth not as man seeth; for man looketh on the outward appearance, but the LORD looketh on the heart."

If you think that merely saying the Lord's prayer is magically protecting you, you are playing games. If you think carrying a Bible under your arm everywhere you go is pleasing God, you are playing games. God is not pleased with our religious trappings.

Games are not for grown-up believers. It is not my job to decide who is playing and who is not, but you can be sure that God knows. Psalm 19:14 says, "Let the words of my mouth, and the meditation of my heart, be acceptable in thy sight, O LORD, my strength, and my redeemer."

"So teach us to number our days, that we may apply our hearts unto wisdom." Psalm 90:12

"Finally, brethren, whatsoever things are true, whatsoever things are honest, whatsoever things are just, whatsoever things are pure, whatsoever things are lovely, whatsoever things are of good report; if there be any virtue, and if there be any praise, think on these things." Philippians 4:8

The Horseshoe Crab

If you heard that horseshoe crab blood is a necessary medical marvel, would you believe the story? It is true. Companies capture millions of crabs, take part of their blood, and release them back into the ocean. Fifteen thousand dollars is the going price for a single quart of this precious substance.

The unique blue blood of this crab distinguishes dangerous bacteria in injectable drugs, implantable medical devices, and hospital instruments. As one conservationist put it, "Every man, woman, and child and domestic animal on this planet that uses medical services is connected to the horseshoe crab." Many readers are possibly living today because of a little crab.

This interesting story brings to our attention another necessary and irreplaceable blood. The Christian church knows or should know the value of the precious blood of Jesus. Acts 20:28 says, "Take heed therefore unto yourselves, and to all the flock, over the which the Holy Ghost hath made you overseers, to feed the church of God, which he hath purchased with his own blood."

The Bible tells us that without the shedding of His blood there is no remission of sins. If Jesus did not bleed on the cross, rise again, and then take that blood to Heaven to put on the mercy seat, then we would be lost in our sins. I Peter 1:18-19 says, "Forasmuch as ye know that ye were not redeemed with corruptible things, as silver and gold... but with the precious blood of Christ, as of a lamb without blemish and without spot."

The medical marvel of the horseshoe crab is nothing to the spiritual marvel of Jesus. "In whom we have redemption through his blood, even the forgiveness of sins." Put your faith and trust in Him today. Let His blood do a miracle in your life. This pastor has experienced it!

Shadows of Life

Standing here at Heritage Baptist Church in Jefferson on a July evening, with the sun setting behind our buildings, it is amazing to view the enormous shadow that our church makes. Have you ever been fascinated with shadows? This writer has ever since he was a child, and still is.

Shadows can affect you for good or bad. In the fall, football game outcomes can be affected as the afternoon shadows lengthen over the playing field. A shadow can shelter you from the hot sun, it can bring fear in the night, or it can even win or lose a sporting event.

The Psalmist wrote in 23:4, "Yea, though I walk through the valley of the shadow of death, I will fear no evil: for thou art with me; thy rod and thy staff they comfort me." Even in the darkest shadow the child of God can find great comfort.

A few years ago, in a visit to Grand Canyon National Park, my family found great joy in watching the birds fly over. While watching them fly, it was amazing to see their shadow on the floor of the canyon. The shadow of one bird could cover an extraordinary amount of ground on the canyon floor. It reminds us of Psalm 17:8; "Keep me as the apple of the eye, hide me under the shadow of thy wings."

If one bird's shadow could cover that much of the Grand Canyon, and our church building shadow could cover our church property, how much more can His shadow protect us? Whatever you are going through now, he can protect you.

Psalms 57:1 says, "Be merciful unto me, O God, be merciful unto me: for my soul trusteth in thee: yea, in the shadow of thy wings will I make my refuge, until these calamities be overpast." Trust in Him today and get under the shadow of His wings.

"How excellent is thy lovingkindness, O God! therefore the children of men put their trust under the shadow of thy wings." Psalm 36:7

"Be merciful unto me, O God, be merciful unto me: for my soul trusteth in thee: yea, in the shadow of thy wings will I make my refuge, until these calamities be overpast." Psalm 57:1

The Cupbearer Called

While reading the book of Nehemiah, this pastor was impacted again by the devotion Nehemiah exhibited toward the work that God had directed him to do. He was not a preacher or prophet, but a simple cupbearer to the king. This usually meant he drank first so that if the drink had poison, he would die and not the king.

God touched the cupbearer's heart about the state of the Jews, and he miraculously opened the door for Nehemiah to do something about the walls of Jerusalem. He even received the blessing, soldiers, and financial backing of the king himself.

It was not all ease in Zion, though. In fact, none of the work was easy. It was hard travel, heavy labor, and it was made even more difficult by their enemies constantly plotting their destruction. They had to work with a tool in one hand and a weapon in the other.

His enemies tried everything they could do to stop him. They even wanted to have a work stoppage so that they could "talk." Nehemiah 6:3-4 says, "And I sent messengers unto them, saying, I am doing a great work, so that I cannot come down: why should the work cease, whilst I leave it, and come down to you? Yet they sent unto me four times after this sort; and I answered them after the same manner."

Nehemiah would finish the work, and ultimately serve as governor in the city or Jerusalem. This story should encourage us to stand for God today. Galatians 5:1 says, "Stand fast therefore in the liberty wherewith Christ hath made us free, and be not entangled again with the yoke of bondage." Whatever God has for you, it will be worth completing.

Paul wrote near the end of his life, "But none of these things move me, neither count I my life dear unto myself, so that I might finish my course with joy, and the ministry, which I have received of the Lord Jesus, to testify the gospel of the grace of God."

"Pray as though everything depended on God. Work as though everything depended on you."-- Augustine

The Bible Says That Jesus is God

Are you certain that Jesus Christ is the Son of God? Without this belief there is no salvation, so that makes this especially important to your future.

Jesus has always been God. Jesus was not a newcomer when he came as a baby in Bethlehem. John 1:1 says, "In the beginning was the Word, and the Word was with God, and the Word was God." John 1:14a states, "And the Word was made flesh, and dwelt among us..." In the beginning, Jesus already existed.

Jesus was God in human form. False teachers teach that Jesus did not have a real body, but the Bible says otherwise. 1 John 1:1 tells us; "That which was from the beginning, which we have heard, which we have seen with our eyes, which we have looked upon, and our hands have handled, of the Word of life." Jesus was not a spirit or an illusion. John knew what he was talking about because he was with him for three years. Jesus is God! Jesus Himself tells us in John 10:30, "I and my Father are one."

We must know Jesus personally. Some people think they would believe in Jesus if they could see a sign or miracle, but Jesus says we are more blessed if we believe without seeing. John 20:29 says, "Jesus saith unto him, Thomas, because thou hast seen me, thou hast believed: blessed are they that have not seen, and yet have believed."

If the Bible will not convince you, nothing will. Jesus is the only way to eternal life. Have you trusted in Him? If not, why not turn to Him today? 2 Corinthians 6:2b says, "...behold, now is the accepted time; behold, now is the day of salvation." Proverbs 3:5 says, "Trust in the LORD with all thine heart; and lean not unto thine own understanding."

From the Diamond to the Bush

Bobby Bonner

Bobby Bonner grew up in southwest Texas in a town called Leakey. He was from a poor family and was the youngest of four children. As a young man he wanted to become a major league baseball player more than anything else.

Bonner excelled at sports, and ultimately received a full scholarship to play shortstop at Texas A&M. In four seasons he set 19 records and led the team to four College World Series appearances. In 1978, the Baltimore Orioles drafted "Iron Man" Cal Ripken in the second round and Bonner in the third round.

Also in 1978, while playing in the minor leagues, Bonner trusted Christ as his Savior at a local church. This decision would change the course of his life. He ultimately would play in the major leagues for Baltimore, but God had something bigger for him than baseball. At 28 years old, at the prime of his career, Bonner walked away from baseball.

In 1986, Bonner surrendered his life to go to Zambia, Africa as a missionary. Since that time, his ministry has seen thousands of people come to the Lord. He has had malaria 19 times, black water fever, and has been chased by rhinos and hippos. He has had king cobras try to get into his house and been spit on by spitting cobras.

Bonner said this about Africa, "My desire is to evangelize, plant churches, and disciple those who have been born again. What a plan! What a place! What a God!" God used a former major league player to start over 200 churches in seven different countries. Every meeting with Brother Bonner will leave a forever impression on you.

A Man Who Changed Lives

Dr. V. Ben Kendrick

All of his 81 years of life, Dr. Vernard Ben Kendrick lived missions.

In 1949, he and his wife Nina began serving in what was then French Equatorial Africa, now Central African Republic and Chad. He served full-time on the field until 1970, but he never retired from missions.

As a teenager, this preacher was so blessed to read and reread Dr Kendrick's missionary books. *Buried Alive for Christ* especially touched my heart in a significant way. His books are wonderful reading for anyone considering missionary work, especially in a closed or third-world country.

This pastor met him in the 1990's while in seminary at Indiana Baptist College. As a missions major, it was a privilege to take every class that he taught. His love for reaching the world was easy to see. The stories of God working in miraculous ways on the mission field firmly planted in my mind the great power of God.

I remember the time he stood in chapel and read a sermon. It was the first time I had ever seen this done, but it was powerful, and the altar filled with young people dedicating themselves to the Lord.

I traveled with him on a preaching trip in Minnesota in 1999. What an unforgettable time. He never met a young man or woman who he did not see potential in, and he willingly invested in their life. His investment in my life was personal and powerful.

When Brother Ben passed away on July 13, 2009, I got in my car and drove 800 miles to attend his funeral. Never a man has walked the earth who touched my life more than this man. He changed the course of my life for the better, and I am thankful for the opportunity to tell him so.

Psalm 34:8 says, "O taste and see that the LORD is good: blessed is the man that trusteth in him."

"God had an only Son and He made Him
a missionary."– David Livingstone

The Tract Man
Evangelist Bruce DeLange

Evangelist Bruce DeLange's influence over my life is long-lasting. Have you ever met him? If so, you probably would remember, and most likely never forget. He probably gave you and several others around you a gospel tract!

A few years back Brother DeLange and I went out distributing tracts on a sunny day in Lebanon, Ohio. He took me to a business district and said, "You take one side of the street, and I will take the other." Honestly, I was a little intimidated and spent more time watching him. While I looked on, he went inside a bank, gave the lady at the front desk a gospel tract, and asked her how many people worked there. The number was over twenty, so he counted out a stack and gave to the woman with an assignment. Pass these out to everyone that worked there. As he walked out the door, she was making her way through the bank passing out tracts!

If you go to eat with him, he will witness to the server and all the tables in the area. He might even sing a song and get the attention of the entire restaurant. All for the purpose of sharing the gospel.

When he preaches, he will ask, "How many of you went by the tract rack and gathered up your supply for this week?" and "How many have tracts in their pocket right now?" Then he often will state, "The proof is in the puddin'" and "Even if you cannot talk 'good', you can still hand someone a gospel tract."

When God called our family to work with him in the tract ministry, my wife said, "How can we ever be like Brother DeLange?" The simple answer is that we could not be like him but we can do our best to imitate his love for lost souls.

Charles Spurgeon stated, "When preaching and private talk are not available, you need to have a tract ready...Get good striking tracts, or none at all. But a touching gospel tract may be the seed of eternal life. Therefore, do not go out without your tracts."

"Then he said unto them, Go your way, eat the fat, and drink the sweet, and send portions unto them for whom nothing is prepared: for *this* day *is* holy unto our Lord: neither be ye sorry; for the joy of the LORD is your strength." Nehemiah 8:10

Purity Pays

Regardless of what the world tells us, and no matter how the Devil blinds us, purity still pays big dividends in God's eyes. We live in a generation of people that have lost their blush and have turned their hearts and thoughts toward things that do not please God. TV and media daily bombard us with sexual sins, immorality, and anti-God propaganda. I am here to lift high the Bible which tells us that purity still pays.

Purity pays with an unblemished body. Sin brings death and the judgment of God. The Bible says that when "Lust is conceived, it bringeth forth death." Sin will destroy you, and it will make you old before your time. I wish the fancy billboards along our highways would show the true end of what sin does. We need to understand that we are facing a tricky adversary. 2 Corinthians 2:11, "Lest Satan should get an advantage of us: for we are not ignorant of his devices."

Purity pays with an undefiled heart. Jesus called the Pharisees of his day hypocrites. They were clean on the outside, but wicked inside. Too many in our midst are becoming that way. Proverbs 4:23 tells us, "Keep thy heart with all diligence; for out of it are the issues of life." We can make a lot of excuses and hide our problems from almost everyone, but God knows. "Ye are they which justify yourselves before men, but God knoweth the heart." (Luke 16:15)

Purity also pays in an unusual wisdom. Psalm 111:10, "The fear of the Lord is the beginning of wisdom." Closeness and submissiveness to God impart wisdom. If your heart is cluttered with the world and its junk, you will not have wisdom when it comes to the things of God. Your life will not have room for church, Bible study, and prayer. We need to do some closet and heart cleaning and make room for the wisdom that matters. Matthew 5:8, "Blessed are the pure in heart, for they shall see God."

"The statutes of the LORD *are* right, rejoicing the heart:
the commandment of the LORD *is* pure, enlightening
the eyes." Psalms 19:8

Protect Your Purity

Job 31:1 says, "I made a covenant with mine eyes; why then should I think upon a maid?" The Hebrew word for covenant is *berit*, meaning "an alliance or pledge." Make this alliance or pledge to God and others to help you be accountable.

Many Christians today struggle because of the lack of a covenant. They let their eyes go wherever they want them to go, with no restrictions. Many believers waste hours of their time feasting their eyes on pornographic material and watch too many shows which are destructive to their relationship with God.

Job made a covenant with his eyes that he would not allow them to dwell upon any woman. The language here is that he solemnly resolved not to do it. Men, you can never be too guarded on this subject, especially in this digital age. We need all the guards in place that we can have.

Have you made a covenant with God regarding your purity? Psalms 101:3 says, "I will set no wicked thing before mine eyes: I hate the work of them that turn aside; it shall not cleave to me." We serve a pure and holy God, and you cannot have a right relationship with Him while entertaining wickedness in your heart. Matthew 5:8 says, "Blessed are the pure in heart: for they shall see God."

Do you have accountability partners in your life? It is important to surround yourself with strong believers that will help you stay right with God. Proverbs 27:17 says, "Iron sharpeneth iron; so a man sharpeneth the countenance of his friend." We all need some friends that will sharpen us in the things of God.

The old saying is true: "Sin will take you further than you want to go, keep you longer than you want to stay, and cost you more than you want to pay." Protect your purity, because the more it gets damaged, the harder it is to restore. Start today by making a covenant with your eyes before God and seeking a godly friend that will help you stay right.

> "I would sooner be holy than happy if the two things could be divorced. Were it possible for a man always to sorrow and yet to be pure, I would choose the sorrow if I might win the purity, for to be free from the power of sin, to be made to love holiness, is true happiness." — Charles Hadden Spurgeon

Bleeding Scripture

This world gets increasingly chaotic, and danger to our spiritual and physical well-being is ever-present. How can we protect ourselves? We need a shield! Proverbs 30:5 says, "Every word of God is pure: he is a shield unto them that put their trust in him."

A medieval shield was a broad piece of armor made of rigid material and carried for safety against hurled or thrusted weapons. The Bible is the same kind of shield to us in these times of peril. Of course, it is an offensive weapon as well (a Sword) but the Scripture is a wonderful defense for the Christian when used properly.

Have you put your trust in God? It is most important. Ephesians 6:16 says, "Above all, taking the shield of faith, wherewith ye shall be able to quench all the fiery darts of the wicked."

The only way we can survive the wickedness of the time we live is the Word of God. John Bunyan was an English writer and Puritan preacher best remembered for writing *Pilgrim's Progress*. He suffered a long prison term just for preaching the Bible. To go free, all John Bunyan had to do was make one promise. He must agree not to preach anymore. Bunyan's simple answer: "If I was out of prison today, I would preach the gospel again tomorrow by the help of God." He spent twelve years in prison for his faith.

How could a man stand that firm on his principles? Charles Spurgeon said, "If you cut him, {John Bunyan} he'd bleed Scripture!"

The Psalmist wrote, "Thou art my hiding place and my shield: I hope in thy word." What are you using for a shield to get you through these uncertain times? Anything but the Bible is going to get a person in serious trouble.

The Bible does you no good sitting on your shelf, or even in your lap for church services. 2 Timothy 2:15 challenges us to "Study to shew thyself approved unto God, a workman that needeth not to be ashamed, rightly dividing the word of truth."

Old timers said, "You can't get blood out of a turnip." The question is, if we "cut" you, would you "bleed" Scripture?

Reaching the Whole World

The gospel of Mark 16:15 says, "Go ye into all the world, and preach the gospel to every creature." Sounds like an impossible task, doesn't it? When we think about it, we realize that God would not have told us to do something that He did not want us to accomplish. Let me give you three ways that we can get the Good News to all the world.

One, we can pray. Philippians 4:6 says, "Be careful for nothing; but in every thing by prayer and supplication with thanksgiving let your request be made known unto God." We need to pray for laborers to be sent. We need to pray for pastors, preachers, Sunday school teachers, and other leaders. We need to pray for our church that God would raise up new soldiers that will go and serve. I Peter 4:7 says, "But the end of all things is at hand: be ye therefore sober, and watch unto prayer."

Two, we can participate. Church will not ever grow without participation. People will not be converted without participation. II Corinthians 4:3 says, "But if our gospel be hid, it is hid to them that are lost." Let's all do our part to reach those around us!

Three, we can pay. We cannot all personally go to all the parts of the world with the gospel message, but we can personally give to help send folks that are able to go. II Corinthians 9:7 says, "Every man according as he purposeth in his heart, so let him give; not grudgingly, or of necessity: for God loveth a cheerful giver."

If the church would rise up, I believe that every person can still hear the gospel message. I am thankful that I got to hear it, but do we care about those who have never heard? Jude 1:22 says, "And of some have compassion, making a difference." We can make a difference!

Does Anyone Fast Anymore?

Mark 9:29 says, "And he {Jesus} said unto them, This kind can come forth by nothing, but by prayer and fasting." We understand the power of fasting, but when was the last time you heard about someone doing it? Jesus spoke these words to the disciples, who could not carry out the work they thought they could do.

A few years ago, this pastor did a survey with his adult Bible class members at church. One of the questions was, "Have you ever fasted?" Another question was, "If yes, when was the last time you did fast?" Out of dozens of responses, only two had ever fasted, and both had not for many years. What spiritual things are not being accomplished?

Matthew 17:21 says, "Howbeit this kind goeth not out but by prayer and fasting." The word "fast" or "a fasting" is *tsom* in the Hebrew and *nesteia* in the Greek language. The Hebrew translation would be "not to eat." The Greek interpretation is "no food."

The importance of fasting cannot be overstated. It is the process of denying ourselves something to reach the throne of God. Fasting is a way to show God how serious we are about our relationship with Him. Those hunger pains help remind us of what we are sacrificing for.

There are many ways to fast, but all of them have great potential to help you grow spiritually. Fasting and praying can permanently change your life. Jesus Himself spent many days fasting when He was in His earthly ministry. Fasting should glorify God not self. Never should it be an emotional experience for a selfish cause. God will honor the Christian who is truly seeking Him. Psalms 105:4 says, "Seek the LORD, and his strength: seek his face evermore."

> "Prayer is reaching out after the unseen; fasting is letting go of all that is seen and temporal. Fasting helps express, deepen, confirm the resolution that we are ready to sacrifice anything, even ourselves to attain what we seek for the kingdom of God."--Andrew Murray

Giving or Receiving?

A recent survey asked Americans what they would do for $10 million dollars. Some said they would abandon all their friends. Some alleged they would murder a stranger or withhold evidence so a murderer could go free. Many responded they would give up their citizenship, and a few reported they would even have a sex-change operation.

You can almost feel the greed of these people who answered the survey's questions. If they were willing to do all these things to get some money, you know they would not be very generous with it. Someone said this, "While it is more blessed to give than receive, most are willing to let someone else get the blessing."

II Corinthians 9:7 tells us, "Every man according as he purposeth in his heart, so let him give; not grudgingly, or of necessity: for God loveth a cheerful giver." The Bible tells the Christian to give joyfully and generously.

Generous giving is a genuine form of worship. King David said: "What shall I render to the Lord for all his benefits towards me?" Giving is an amazing way of showing our love to God and seeing how He uses us to impact others. When we give, our attitude transforms.

It is true that you can't take anything with you when you die, but you can send it on ahead. Every time we give, we are investing in heavenly rewards that will last forever.

The Bible teaches that if you have material possessions and you see a brother or sister in need and have no pity, how can the love of God be in you? It is not hard to find people with greater needs than we have, so where is our heart directing us to give? Generous actions speak louder than words.

"A poor person isn't he who has little,
but he who needs a lot." — Proverb

"If your only goal is to become rich, you
will never achieve it."—John D. Rockefeller

"One gains by losing self for others and not by
hoarding for oneself." — Watchman Nee

Lost Connection

Social media is an amazing tool for connecting with the past. Someone this pastor has not seen since kindergarten and who lives 1,052 miles away sent a message. This was our first communication in almost 40 years! Have you ever had something like this happen?

She said, "I always remembered I had a friend named Seth but didn't know his last name. I just found the class picture in a binder & realized my mom had written your name on the back behind your picture..." As an only child, she shared, "That may be why I always remembered I had a friend named Seth. You might have been my first official friend."

This was an amazing thing to have happen, and it was thrilling to connect with someone from that part of my life. This event reminded me of another Friend. Almost 40 years ago, during the same period of my life, I connected with this "one-of-a-kind" Friend. During all these years, He has never left my side. He has been faithful through every circumstance and situation. That Friend is Jesus Christ.

Social media is great for connecting with friends from around the world, but do not neglect the Friend "...that sticketh closer than a brother." He will be with you when you turn off the computer, when you go through the dark times of your life, and when you lose loved ones to the grave.

Have you "connected" with Jesus? Romans 10:13 says, "For whosoever shall call upon the name of the Lord shall be saved." He is just a "call" away from entering your heart forever. Maybe you have lost connection with Him and you need to reconnect today.

Psalm 107:27-30 says, "They reel to and fro...and are at their wits' end. Then they cry unto the LORD in their trouble, and he bringeth them out of their distresses. He maketh the storm a calm, so that the waves thereof are still. Then are they glad because they be quiet; so he bringeth them unto their desired haven."

How to Pray for Your Pastor.

How do you pray for your pastor? Romans 15:30 says, "Now I beseech you, brethren, for the Lord Jesus Christ's sake, and for the love of the Spirit, that ye strive together with me in your prayers to God for me."

Pastors need prayer as they maneuver through the intricacies of modern ministry. Race issues, society problems, family breakdowns, and politics are things that a pastor must face daily. The pastor is expected to have the right answers. As a pastor I hopes this list will help you in praying for your minister.

Preparation of Sermons. Your pastor wants the sermon being prepared to impact hearts and meet the needs of the listeners. Pray that God will give great wisdom to your leader during the study time.

Physical Situations. Pray for your pastor to have good health, good relationships, good travel, and even that the internet and computer will function properly. These things can greatly impact ministry.

Protection Spiritually. Satan does not want the pastor to have a powerful and impactful message. Satan is the enemy of everything right. Pray that God will protect from this pitfall.

Progress Spiritually. Your pastor is still growing in the Lord. Pray that the growth will be positive and that your mentor will live for God in a pleasing way.

Performance of Schedule. The pastor cannot do the job effectively with distractions. Pray that God will keep the problems at a minimum in the life of your minister. A sore throat, a family issue, or an overbooked calendar can all mess with the mind and spirit.

Power of the Sermon. This is so important! Pray that the message will do what God intends for it. Pray for fruit in the lives of the hearers and surrender in the hearts of the lost.

It is so important to pray for your pastor that God will work and direct in the ministry. Your prayers could make an eternal difference. Even when you do not know exactly how to pray, just pray! Romans 8:26 says, "Likewise the Spirit also helpeth our infirmities: for we know not what we should pray for as we ought: but the Spirit itself maketh intercession for us with groanings which cannot be uttered."

How to Pray for Your Church

How do you pray for your church? 2 Thessalonians 1:11 says, "Wherefore also we pray always for you, that our God would count you worthy of this calling, and fulfil all the good pleasure of his goodness, and the work of faith with power."

During these chaotic years, it has become increasingly obvious that the church needs prayer. The Devil is probably not a fan of your congregation and minister. Hopefully, the following list will help you pray for your assembly in a clearer way.

Accord. How we need to pray for unity in our churches. Psalm 133:1 says, "Behold, how good and how pleasant it is for brethren to dwell together in unity!" Pray that God will unify us around the truth and bring us closer to Him in the process.

Attitude. Pray for your church to have the right attitude in the hearts, in the homes, and in the community. From the senior pastor to the most recent member, attitude is important. Make this a regular matter of prayer.

Attendance. Recent events have exposed this need in a big way. We need to pray that God will bring our world, our country, and our church back to the house of God. Hebrews 10:25 says, "Not forsaking the assembling of ourselves together, as the manner of some is; but exhorting one another: and so much the more, as ye see the day approaching."

Advancement. Retreat is never an option, nor should foolish pride be an option. Without God's help the church will never advance. People still need Christ, so the church must go forward. Pray that your assembly can advance and do more in the coming days.

Obviously, everything that needs prayer is not on mentioned, but it is a good place to start. Add to this list as you see fit, but fervently pray for your church that God will use it in our generation.

2 Thessalonians 3:1 says, "Finally, brethren, pray for us, that the word of the Lord may have free course, and be glorified, even as it is with you."

We Are All Dedicated to Something

A notable minister of the past, Vance Havner said, "A wife who is 85 percent faithful to her husband is not faithful at all. There is no such thing as part-time loyalty to Jesus Christ." There is a lot of truth in that little quote.

Sports would cease to exist without dedicated fans. They fill the stadiums and buy merchandise. Music stars would have no platform on which to sing and perform without dedicated followers. Dedication is essential to almost every business and company no matter what their product.

Considering what the Bible tells Christ-followers about Jesus, how can we not be dedicated? Someone said this: "God does not require a man to have one talent, three talents, or five talents. He only requires that a man be faithful with whatever he has been given."

The Babylonians captured young Daniel and carried him far from home and family. It would have been easy to have gone his own way, yet the trials he faced seemed only to make him more dedicated to the Lord. The Bible says that as a youth Daniel purposed in his heart to follow the Lord. This decision many years later would still stand when Daniel had to face the lions' den.

Are you truly dedicated to the things of God? Psalm 34:3 says, "O magnify the LORD with me, and let us exalt his name together." You can never learn and experience the joy of putting God first in everything until you start putting God first in everything.

Are you struggling with a dedication to God, to the church, or in your marriage? Dedication is an act, not just something you have spoken. Dedication should an essential part of Christian life. There were times when the only thing that will keep us going is our act of dedication.

> "But Daniel purposed in his heart that he would not defile himself with the portion of the king's meat, nor with the wine which he drank: therefore he requested of the prince of the eunuchs that he might not defile himself." Daniel 1:8

> "Create in me a clean heart, O God; and renew a right spirit within me." Psalms 51:10

Thanks to God

Psalm 100 says, "Know ye that the LORD he is God: it is he that hath made us, and not we ourselves; we are his people, and the sheep of his pasture. Enter into his gates with thanksgiving, and into his courts with praise: be thankful unto him and bless his name."

These familiar words give clear evidence for the case of thankfulness. He is God, and really nothing else needs added. Simply be thankful for God Himself. David said in II Samuel 7:22, "For there is not like thee, neither is there any God beside thee."

Not only is He God, but He is a good God. "For the Lord is good; his mercy is everlasting; and his truth endureth to all generations." While God's goodness is constant and universal, it is good as a people and as a country to set aside a Thanksgiving Day to commemorate His goodness. God is good, God is merciful and God is faithful. Whether you were a Pilgrim, or you are a Baby Boomer, Millennial, or Generation Z, you are given reasons for thankfulness to Him. No matter what generation comes and goes, God's greatness extends far beyond.

What a joy being made one of His people! He is our Creator, but He is so much more. We are His workmanship, created in Christ Jesus, which gives us plenty of reason to praise and thank Him. He is our Shepherd who provides for us and guides us through life.

The Pilgrims had just gotten through a tough year in 1621. They had very little, but they were thankful. Many will gather regularly around tables loaded with delicious food but with little thankfulness. Do not be like that. Let us be thankful to a great God that has given us so much.

Thanksgiving in a Pickle

Jonah was in the belly of a big fish, when out of his mouth came these words: "But I will sacrifice unto thee with the voice of thanksgiving; I will pay that that I have vowed. Salvation is of the LORD."

Recent times have been a pickle for many folks. Thankfulness is harder when you are in a pickle, but it can be done. Jonah was in a mess, and yet still expressed thanksgiving. How can we still be thankful during the "pickle" times of our lives?

Let us be thankful for a ready God. God prepared a big fish, a gourd, a worm, and wind. He prepared a city that needed Jesus and a man to take them the message. God prepares the way in your life as well. Psalm 23:5 says, "Thou preparest a table before me in the presence of mine enemies: thou anointest my head with oil; my cup runneth over."

Let us be thankful for a responding God. Jonah deserved the mess that he was in and did not deserve a response from God. This pastor is thankful that God loves us enough to hear us even when we do not deserve it.

Let us be thankful for a rescuing God. God brought Jonah out of the stomach of a fish, and God can bring us through a year like we have experienced. Psalm 34:22 says, "The LORD redeemeth the soul of his servants: and none of them that trust in him shall be desolate."

Let us be thankful for a rich God. Ephesians 2:4 says, "But God, who is rich in mercy, for his great love wherewith he loved us." Let us be thankful for a God of second chances. He is rich in his mercy toward us all the time. Let us be thankful people--- even in a pickle! Yes, there is much still to be thankful for!

Quarantined

When contracting Covid-19 in 2020, the virus that has swept across our world, this writer and his family practiced quarantine. Although restrictive, the redeeming factor is that it did not last forever. It was a temporary setback that soon passed.

The Bible tells the story of many who were quarantined in much worse situations. The lepers of ancient times knew that there was no cure. They quarantined in leper colonies, waiting to die.

This is what makes the story in Luke 17 so special. "And as he {Jesus} entered into a certain village, there met him ten men that were lepers, which stood afar off: And they lifted up their voices, and said, Jesus, Master, have mercy on us. And when he saw them, he said unto them, Go shew yourselves unto the priest. And it came to pass, that, as they went, they were cleansed."

This was a life changing moment for these ten men. No longer were they quarantined for life, but now they were free to go back to their families, their jobs, and their life. What a wonderful story with a happy ending!

The story concludes this way: "And one of them, when he saw that he was healed, turned back, and with a loud voice glorified God, and he fell down on his face at his feet, giving him thanks: and he was a Samaritan."

Jesus shows amazement that only one came back to glorify Him and give Him thanks. He says, "Arise, go thy way: thy faith hath made thee whole." Ten men were freed from quarantine. One of them received much more.

Because of his faith in the Lord Jesus, this Samaritan obtained freedom of his soul and eternal life. I pray that you have experienced this freedom as well. If you experience salvation, they can quarantine your body, but never your soul.

> "Neither is there salvation in any other: for there is none other name under heaven given among men, whereby we must be saved." Acts 4:12

Great Grandparents

Proverbs 17:6 says, "Children's children {Grandkids} are the crown of old men; and the glory of children are their fathers."

Every September, Grandparents Day is celebrated, and this event brings back many memories of my grandparents. I did not know my mom's parents very well, but I did get to spend a lot of time with my dad's parents. My brother and I always looked forward to time with them. They were godly people who enjoyed life, appreciated each other, and loved to spend time with us.

Take time for your grandkids. You will be a helpful source of strength, information, and wisdom. Grandchildren will learn family history and of times long ago, and how to live a thankful and full life. As a young child, I looked at my grandparents and saw superheroes.

Psalm 103:17 says, "But the mercy of the LORD is from everlasting to everlasting upon them that fear him, and his righteousness unto children's children." This verse tells us that it is important for grandparents to walk with God. A good grandparent will say as the Psalmist, "I have been young, and now am old; yet have I not seen the righteous forsaken, nor his seed begging bread."

Remember, the daily decisions you make are affecting not just your children, but your grandchildren as well. Proverbs 16:31 challenges, "The hoary {gray} head is a crown of glory, if it be found in the way of righteousness." Your walk with God in the latter years of your life will leave a lasting impression on those little eyes.

What an honor to speak at both of my grandparents' funerals and this pastor had nothing but praise to share about their long lives. My personal prayer is to be an excellent grandparent when the time comes.

Rudy Giuliani said, "What children need most are the essentials that grandparents provide in abundance. They give unconditional love, kindness, patience, humor, comfort, lessons in life. And, most importantly, cookies."

"One generation shall praise thy works to another, and shall declare thy mighty acts." Psalm 145:4

Camouflage Christians

Deer season comes every fall, and everywhere you look, camouflage is in style. This guy thinks it is classy and elegant year around, but that is beside the point! When hunting season begins, hunters start thinking about how to blend in.

Camouflage is good for hunting, but it is never good for the Christian. Why? Because we are children of the light. The Devil, however, is all about blending in. Ephesians 6:11 says, "Put on the whole armor of God, that ye may be able to stand against the wiles of the devil." He is tricky, and the Bible says that he conceals himself as an "angel of light."

Believers should not camouflage but shine forth. Philippians 2:15 tells us, "That ye may be blameless and harmless, the sons of God, without rebuke, in the midst of a crooked and perverse nation, among whom ye shine as lights in the world." Jesus said, "Ye are the light of the world."

If we hide the light that is within us, how will the light shine in this dark world? The sad answer is that it will not. If there was ever a time that Christians need to shine, it is now.

When the lights go off in a cave, it gets really dark. Even the smallest light shines bright in those conditions. The same opportunity is available for a Christian in these days. It is not hard to shine brightly if we will let Jesus shine through us.

During hunting season, wear the camouflage clothes, conceal your scent, and even paint your face to blend into your hunting blind. Just do not be a camouflage Christian. Ephesians 5:8 says, "For ye were sometimes darkness, but now are ye light in the Lord: walk as children of light."

Opening Weekend

Psalm 42:1 says, "As the hart {deer} panteth after the water brooks, so panteth my soul after thee, O God." The opening of deer season is special for many folks and is eagerly anticipated by hunters of all ages. Someone said this: "Roses are red, violets are blue, attention all deer, I'm coming for you!"

Some folks across the country think that East Texans don't appreciate nature because we hunt, fish, and cut trees, but for most of us, nothing could be further from the truth. Psalm 8:8-9 says, "The fowl of the air, and the fish of the sea, and whatsoever passeth through the paths of the seas. O LORD our Lord, how excellent is thy name in all the earth."

Natural beauty surrounds us everywhere we look. We may not have the incredible fall foliage of areas north and east of us, but we have a lot of other beautiful sights here in this area. It is worthy of a prayer of thanksgiving lifted from a hunting stand on a fall weekend. Psalm 116:12 says, "What shall I render unto the Lord for all his benefits toward me?"

The question is are you as excited about Jesus as you are your new bow or hunting stand? Will you skip church on a Sunday to chase after that trophy buck? One Sunday in a Bible teaching church is worth more than all the deer that will gather around your feeder or food plot.

Enjoy your time hunting, but do not forget how important the Lord is. Without Him hunting would be impossible. I wear camouflage but my faith should never be hidden. Romans 1:16 says, "For I am not ashamed of the gospel of Christ, for it is the power of God unto salvation to every one that believeth."

Reflecting Jesus in Our Race

Too many people do not finish their race. They give up, give in, or just plain quit. Nowhere in the Bible are we promised that the Christian life is going to be easy. In fact, often the opposite is true.

That seems to be the idea in the book of Hebrews. These Christians endured a terrible time of trial and persecution. In light of that, the writer is attempting to encourage these weary, hurting believers to be faithful to the Lord and to continue to run their race.

Hebrews 12:1-2, "Wherefore seeing we also are compassed about with so great a cloud of witnesses, let us lay aside every weight, and the sin which doth so easily beset us, and let us run with patience the race that is set before us."

Jesus is our great example of a race finisher.

The author of Hebrews isn't talking about a 100-yard dash. Instead, the author is referring to a marathon. A marathon is a race that requires endurance and preparation. I know that I am in no physical shape to run in a marathon, but I can be in the kind of spiritual shape it takes to run the Christian race.

When there is a race to be run, the wise runner must make careful preparations. The same is true in a spiritual race as well. We will never reach our fullest potential for the Lord until we are willing to make the preparations and sacrifices that are necessary for running the race.

The Bible tells us here that Jesus ran "for the joy that was set before Him" Where is the joy in going to a cross? Where is the joy in dying like a common criminal? Where is the joy in being rejected by people you love? For Jesus, the joy was in what would happen when He finished His race.

We need to come to the place where we are able to look beyond the situations and circumstances of life and envision that day when we will be home with the Savior. My prayer for myself is that when I reach the end of my race I might say with the Apostle Paul, "I have fought a good fight, I have finished my course, I have kept the faith." 2 Tim. 4:7

Reflecting Jesus in Our Urgency

This pastor struggles with urgency — I really do. I tend to put things off until tomorrow. I sleep well at night, and do not worry much about the future. I guess sometimes that is good, but sometimes this attitude gets me in trouble. There are some things that a Christian should be urgent about.

Jesus' disciples struggled with that many times as well. In this brief article, I do not claim to have all the answers, but I want to give you one simple thing that we should have an urgency about.

Simply put, we should be urgent in our obedience. Dragging our feet in obedience can lead to destruction. If we know what is right to do, why wait? John 14:15, "If ye love me, keep my commandments."

Reasons to be urgent in our obedience
1. Because you are thankful for what God has done for you.
2. Because He loves you and you love Him.
3. Because He is Lord.
4. Because you are new creature.
5. Because there is a lost world looking on.
6. Because God rewards obedience.
7. Because you fear God.
8. Because you want your prayers answered.
9. Because sin grieves God.
10. Because you want to live in joy.

My children sing a song and some of the words go like this:

"Obedience is the very best way, to show that you believe. Doing exactly what the Lord commands, and doing it happily. Action is the key, do it immediately, joy you will receive. Obedience is the very best way, to show that you believe."

The Bible says that Jesus was obedient even in His death on the cross. The least that we can do as followers is obey. Let's get busy doing that today.

Reflecting Jesus in our Vision

All of us understand how a reflection works. Anyone that has been near a body of water has seen their own reflection in that water. The question of the day is this: are we reflecting Jesus in our vision?

What in your life is hindering your vision today? Proverbs 29:18, "Where there is no vision, the people perish: but he that keepeth the law, happy is he."

There is great danger in not having a vision. The Bible says that people perish! A vision will not just happen by accident, but takes passion to make your vision a priority.

Do you have a vision for your church? Every pastor in the world would desire that every member has a vision for the cause of their church. Do you have a vision for the services, for the missions, and for the needs? Do you have a vision for your church to continue long after you are gone?

Do you have a vision for hurting people? Matthew 14:14, "And Jesus went forth, and saw a great multitude, and was moved with compassion toward them, and he healed their sick."

Step one-- see the need. Step two--have compassion. Step three -- make a difference. We are faced every day with the same opportunities, and yet because of our lack of vision we never get past step one. Hurting people are all over our community, so will we have a vision for these needs?

Luke 10:2, "Therefore said he unto them, The harvest truly is great, but the labourers are few: pray ye therefore the Lord of the harvest, that he would send forth labourers into his harvest."

Let's get a vision for our neighbors, our town, our state, our country, and our world. Let us reflect the heart and mind of Christ in our vision to make a difference for the kingdom.

Why Read the Bible?

Often, we are told at church that we should read our Bibles. What makes this so necessary? I just go to church and get the same result, right? Here are several reasons why you should read for yourself.

First, it brings wisdom. The Bible is stuffed full of words of wisdom. It holds wisdom about our finances, our future, our families....everything. When we get wisdom, we do better in every area of our life.

Second, it helps us with sin and temptations. We all struggle with this every day of our lives. That is where the Bible comes in. When we read the Scriptures, it strengthens us to overcome temptation.

Third, reading your Bible brings peace. In the business of our daily lives, things can get out of control. Reading the Bible brings everything back into perspective and allows us to focus our attention on what is truly important.

Fourth, the Bible gives direction. Do you feel like you are wandering about and feeling pretty useless? When we read the Bible, God speaks to us, and our purpose can be located within the pages of the Scriptures. His words can give us a route to follow, for the long haul or a temporary situation.

Fifth, it builds a relationship with God. For the believer this should be of utmost importance. Reading our Bibles teaches us much about God. The Bible will help your prayer life. You cannot help but grow closer to God while reading the pages of His Word.

Sixth, it can change your life. Wait, it WILL change your life! If you could have every book in the world, or one copy of the Bible, you would not go wrong picking the Bible! The answer to any problem is sitting in the pages of the Bible. The Bible answers depression, defeat, discouragement. It can change your life every time you open it.

Last of all, it teaches faith, and not religion. How often we get caught up in our church, or our religious beliefs. Your church and religion mean little without faith. Without faith you have no salvation. Without faith you have no walk with God. The Bible teaches faith, and our faith will grow with reading the Word.

The Most Wonderful Time

"It's the Most Wonderful Time of the Year" was written to celebrate some of the traditions many people take part in each year during the Christmas season. This song was released over fifty years ago but remains a much-requested song year after year.

The Christmas season is a great time to gather with family and friends for joyful fellowship, but for many people this is far from the truth. We have folks in our churches and communities that have recently lost dear family members, experienced divorce or separation, or had other chaos in their lives. We live in an imperfect world where things often get completely out of control, and all our certainties suddenly are anything but certain.

Joseph and Mary knew what is was like to have their world turned upside down. In Matthew chapter one, we read about how Joseph was getting ready to marry the woman he loved but was hit with unexpected news and struggled to get a handle on it.

We can only imagine how Joseph must have felt hearing that his future wife was going to have a baby that was not his. He had no idea what to do and was even considering ending his relationship with Mary.

Joseph decided to wait on the Lord. When circumstances come into our lives, we need to wait to hear from God. Isaiah 40:31 says, "But they that wait upon the Lord shall renew their strength; they shall mount up with wings as eagles; they shall run, and not be weary; and they shall walk, and not faint."

At this moment of hopelessness for Joseph, God stepped in. Remember, God always has a plan to bring good out of suffering. As we celebrate each Christmas, we should celebrate the hope that comes with it. That hope is centered on Jesus Christ and why He came to earth. Let all your hope rest upon this truth.

> "We venture to assert, that if there be any day in the year,
> of which we may be pretty sure that it was not the day
> on which the Savior was born, it is the 25th of December.
> Regarding not the day, let us, nevertheless, give thanks to
> God for the gift of His dear Son." — Charles Hadden Spurgeon

Hurting Around the Christmas Tree
Abigail Goodman

Hurting people are everywhere on Christmas. Tragedy, divorce, separation and death are found any direction we look.

A while ago some dear friends lost their 16-year-old daughter suddenly and tragically. How can we celebrate the joy of the season when all we feel is hurt? How can we enjoy the most wonderful time of the year when very little seems wonderful in our lives?

The best verse that comes to mind is Psalm 46:10, "Be still, and know that I am God." The holidays are full of excitement and even chaos, and God is hard to see even in the celebration of Jesus' birth. Sometimes in grief it is the stillness that we dread, yet that is the very time the Lord can speak to our hearts and show peace and comfort. Be still.

When stillness is not an option, reach out to those who are in greater need than ourselves. Often our hurt will make us only inwardly focused. Recognize that hurting people are everywhere and be intentional about finding someone else to help. Romans 12:10,13 says, "Be kindly affectioned one to another with brotherly love; in honour preferring one another; Distributing to the necessity of saints; given to hospitality."

Finally, do not give up hope. Not now...not ever. In the dark moments of our lives, it is easy to feel very overwhelmed.

Jesus came as a baby in a dark time in human history, and He brought so much light that it extends through all of history. He wants to bring light to your life on Christmas. Psalm 39:7 says, "And now, Lord, what wait I for? my hope is in thee." Luke 2:10 says, "And the angel said unto them, Fear not: for, behold, I bring you good tidings of great joy, which shall be to all people."

This devotion was written in loving memory of my friend Abigail Goodman, who passed away on December 3rd, 2019, at the age of 16.

I love and pray regularly for the Goodman family.

"And God shall wipe away all tears from their eyes; and there shall be no more death, neither sorrow, nor crying, neither shall there be any more pain: for the former things are passed away." Revelation 21:4

"For I reckon that the sufferings of this present time are not worthy to be compared with the glory which shall be revealed in us." Romans 8:18

Running The Wrong Race

English runner Omar Ahmed signed up to run the "Great Bristol Run" 10k race in September of 2021. This race started in the same place as a half-marathon, but the paths separated at some point of the event. Ahmed took the wrong way and ended up running in the half-marathon. Not only did he run, but he also won the race four minutes ahead of the nearest competitor.

Marathon organizers disqualified him. The reason they gave was since he was not registered for the half-marathon, he technically could not be the winner.

How many people are running through life thinking they are on the right path?

Hebrews 12:1 says, "Wherefore seeing we also are compassed about with so great a cloud of witnesses, let us lay aside every weight, and the sin which doth so easily beset *us*, and let us run with patience the race that is set before us." Hebrews tells us to run "the race that is set before us." God has a course set for the believer, and we must run His race.

It might seem like we are winning, just as Ahmed was initially declared the winner. Our friends may tell us we are winning. Our family may encourage us onward. Our church family and pastor may even be excitedly cheering us to "victory."

Our life may please us and others who look on, but is it pleasing to God? Hebrews 11:6 tells us, "But without faith *it is* impossible to please *him*: for he that cometh to God must believe that he is, and *that* he is a rewarder of them that diligently seek him."

Somewhere in the middle of the race, Ahmed realized that he was off course, but he decided to continue and finish. Maybe he hoped no one would notice or care. He did so well, so perhaps he felt a reward was appropriate for all the effort he put forth.

God is watching our life, and He cares what course we take. He wants believers in His race. When we stand before Him, it will matter what race we ran. It matters how we run the race. Are you running the race God has for you? In times of doubt, God has a race instruction manual to check with. Psalm 119:105 says, "Thy word *is* a lamp unto my feet, and a light unto my path."

Finish Strong

Each year seems to fly by, and a new year is coming. Before embarking on this fresh start, do not forget there are still a few important days left before the year concludes.

One key to starting the new year well is finishing the old year right. Acts 20:24 says, "But none of these things move me, neither count I my life dear unto myself, so that I might finish my course with joy…" All people have a life course and finishing is one of mankind's greatest achievements.

Derek Redmond is a retired Olympian. During his career, he set records and won medals, but he is most remembered for how he finished a race during the 1992 Olympic Games in Barcelona, when he tore his hamstring mid race. In spite of the injury he continued the race. While limping painfully and with help from his father, he managed to complete a full lap of the track as the crowd stood and cheered. The judges disqualified Derek because of assistance from his dad and officially listed him as "Did Not Finish." Actually, this might have been his greatest finish, becoming an inspiring part of Olympic history.

You may have suffered many trials in the past year, or you may have had a great year of success. Either way, finish this year as strong as you can. Some great ideas for doing that are to attend your church this Sunday, read your Bible, and show love to the One who directs your course. Romans 8:28 says, "And we know that all things work together for good to them that love God, to them who are the called according to his purpose." Like Derek, your finish can inspire and encourage others to do the same.

Made in the USA
Monee, IL
27 September 2023

43514028R00059